COPING WITH POST-TRAUMA STRESS

FRANK PARKINSON is a consultant, trainer and university lecturer, specializing in coping with stress and trauma. He has worked with helpers and victims after many different events, from traffic accidents, assaults, armed robberies and hostage situations to major disasters. He teaches skills of Defusing and Debriefing, works with individuals and groups, and is the author of *Post-Trauma Stress* (Sheldon Press, 1993), *Listening and Helping in the Workplace* (Souvenir Press, 1995) and *Critical Incident Debriefing* (Souvenir Press, 1997). Frank was a clergyman and army chaplain for over 30 years, who trained as a Relate counsellor.

Overcoming Common Problems Series

For a full list of titles please contact
Sheldon Press, Marylebone Road, London NW1 4DU

Overcoming Common Problems Series

Overcoming Common Problems Series

Overcoming Common Problems

Coping With Post-Trauma Stress

Frank Parkinson

Published in Great Britain in 2000 by
Sheldon Press
SPCK
Holy Trinity Church
Marylebone Road
London NW1 4DU

Revised edition 2000

British Library Cataloguing-in-Publication Data

A catalogue record for this book is available from the British Library

ISBN 0–85969–843–2

Typeset by Deltatype Limited, Birkenhead, Merseyside
Printed in Great Britain by
Biddles Ltd, Guildford and King's Lynn

Contents

Introduction

Are you experiencing reactions to some incident in the past, recent or a long time ago, which are disturbing your life and you think there must be something wrong with you? Do you live or work with someone who has had a traumatic experience, perhaps someone you love, and are finding them and their behaviour difficult? Are you a professional helper or rescuer, someone who regularly encounters trauma in your work, and wonder how you would cope if it affected you or a colleague? Have you read about accidents and disasters in the media and the possible effects on individuals, groups and families and wonder what it's all about? Are you a counsellor, clergyman or helper, or simply someone with a general interest in trauma? Perhaps you believe that reactions to a traumatic incident are not normal and that there must be something wrong with you or with those who suffer?

If you are suffering, you might have been shocked and stunned by an experience which has shaken and shattered your world and you don't know what to do. Talking about it to your partner or a friend, 'getting things off your chest' and expressing your emotions might help, but these can be difficult. Have you had the 'eyes glaze over' experience where you talk, but realize that they cannot understand what you have been through or know how you feel? Also, others might think you are weak for not coping, so it's easier to keep your feelings to yourself and suffer in silence.

But what happens when you do push your feelings away and try to forget them? They have a nasty habit of jumping to the surface when you don't want them to or when you thought they had gone away. Buried feelings can come out in bouts of irritability, anger, frustration and depression. Have you considered that the best way forward might be to face up to what has happened? What you have experienced and are going through is now part of you and your life. It will not be easy, but you can reach a stage where it becomes bearable and the memories, although still painful, can emerge without destroying you. You accept that the experience is still there inside, but you know you can cope. When you see the experience not as an enemy to be avoided, but as one you have faced, you can move on. You can achieve this when you:

ix

- understand that the traumatic incident initiated your reactions;
- understand what is happening to you and why;
- believe that your reactions are normal and natural;
- understand how it is affecting those around you;
- use strategies for coping;
- look for and accept help when you need it.

If you have a partner who is experiencing reactions, you also will be finding it difficult to know what to do. There are ways in which you can help and there are right and wrong ways of responding. There is hope and there are pathways through your experiences, even if they are sometimes hard to find or follow, but with understanding and compassion, you can learn to cope. This book can help you find your way, but do not expect to find all the answers here or think that after reading it you will be 'cured'. Traumatic stress is not like having measles. To recover, you need to be determined to work through the experience and make it part of who and what you are. Your daily mantra should be:

> 'I have been in a traumatic accident. I can face up to it and live with it and it will not destroy me. I am not weak or pathetic and I will get through it.'

1

What is Post-Trauma Stress?

What is Post-Trauma Stress? 'Post' means 'after' and 'trauma' comes from a Greek word meaning to wound or hurt. In a medical setting, trauma is used to mean either a physical injury or damage from an accident or operation or an emotional shock which can have lasting psychological and physical effects. 'Post-Trauma' therefore refers to the physical and emotional reactions you might experience after a traumatic incident. However, reactions often occur before and during an incident as well as after it. If you saw someone coming towards you with the obvious intention of attacking you or mugging you, you might tell yourself to stay calm and cool and this could help you to cope and survive. Or you might feel anxious at first, then frozen with disbelief, and the shock finally erupts when it's over. Alternatively, you could be terrified from beginning to end. Once the incident is over, reactions might be temporary and short-lived, where you take a deep breath and say, 'OK. I'm all right now,' or they could persist, intensify and change. Usually, reactions gradually diminish with time and the incident becomes an event in the past which you can live with. You can still recall memories, emotions and feelings, but they are not unduly worrying or upsetting. Sometimes they continue much longer and become intrusive and disturbing and you begin to wonder, 'What's wrong with me?' You have vivid reminders of the incident and it is still going on in your life now. You might even feel that the ways you have reacted must be your fault. 'I was absolutely petrified when that man pointed the gun at me. I still feel frightened and shouldn't be like this.' But it is normal to be afraid when someone points a gun at you and it is normal for these reactions to continue at some level.

Defining the word 'stress' creates problems. It can mean a force or tension applied to an object which might cause it to bend or break, but it can also mean a mentally and physically disrupting pressure or strain placed on an individual, on a group, or even on a family or community. Some people believe that there is no such thing as stress, unless you are weak, while others see it only as the result of a major disaster or horrific incident. One useful way of understanding it is to think of two kinds of stress: 'eu-stress' and 'dys-stress'.

1

Eu-stress

Eu is a Greek prefix meaning good or positive, used in words like euphoria (good feelings), euphonium (good sounding) and eulogy (good words). Eu-stress is 'good-stress': something you experience simply from being alive. Your heart is beating and pumping blood around your body, you are breathing, your digestive system is working and you don't even have to think about it because your autonomic nervous system controls all these activities. Even when you are asleep or anaesthetized, you still have blood pressure and stress in your body. In addition, you have the physical and emotional stresses from your daily life: from relationships, work and whatever is happening around you. You are watching the news on TV. Your blood pressure rises and you become excited and happy, nervous and frightened, angry and upset, depending on what you are viewing. You are under stress, but there is nothing wrong with you. Eu-stress enables you to feel exhilaration and excitement on a roller-coaster, to feel angry when abused, to be frightened and chilled by a horror film and to drive safely in heavy traffic.

The level of stress goes up and down every day and throughout your life, but you usually cope, even when the stress is high. Falling in love involves experiencing many different and powerful emotions, including peaks of happiness and excitement as well as deep anxiety and sadness. But strong emotions are usually the appropriate responses to situations of stress. Without anger, you wouldn't tackle the inequalities and injustices of life and would allow others to walk all over you, but too high a level of anger can result in apoplexy. Feeling guilty can enable you to say you are sorry and put things right, but extreme guilt can lead to suicide. Stress is like the level in a thermometer. As the stress goes up, the level rises, and when the stress reduces, the level falls, and this happens to you every day of your life. Some experiences stimulate you and others depress you, but you cope. Parachutists, mountain climbers and dangerous sports enthusiasts thrive on high levels of excitement and fear, and, even at this level, it is still positive stress. But sometimes the stress rises to a point where reactions are increasingly disturbing and your ability to cope is challenged and diminished.

Dys-stress

A prefix used in our language is 'dys' or 'dis', which means bad or the negative of whatever word follows it: disgrace (bad-grace), disfigured (harmed-appearance) and disable (poor-ability). 'Dys-stress', or distress, is 'bad stress' or stress which you experience or interpret as harmful and hurtful. If the level in the stress-thermometer rises beyond a certain point, eu-stress becomes dys-stress and your physical and emotional reactions intensify. You don't have to ask for these to happen. They just do. Your heart beats faster, you begin to sweat, your muscles feel tense, you have headaches and stomach aches and there is a tightness in your chest. You might deny there is a problem, feel irritable, angry, guilty, anxious, hopeless, frightened, panicky, lose confidence, make mistakes and find difficulty in making decisions.

These are all natural and some of the many possible reactions you might experience, but if the distress continues to rise and intensify, you eventually 'burn out' or 'break down'. You have gone beyond the optimum level for coping and your whole mind and body system begins to collapse. Usually this doesn't happen because, when you know something is wrong, you take a break, go home, rest and relax or do something physical. Even when you have a breakdown you recover, usually after a period of rest with the help of your GP and, sometimes, medication. Also, the level at which eu-stress becomes dys-stress varies from situation to situation and from time to time. You might cope with or ignore your surly and inconsiderate colleague one day, but the next day you can't stand it and you lose your temper. How have you coped with stress in your life? Have you mellowed with the years or are you someone who is almost constantly angry with everything and everyone? Being angry can enable you to cope better with difficult people and situations, even if others find it difficult to cope with you! If you are being unfairly treated in a shop or restaurant what do you do? Do you cringe into a polite shell, or do you stand up for your rights? 'How is your meal, madam?' 'Er, all right, thank you,' you reply, when the plate is cold, the meal disgusting and inside you are seething with anger. There is a time for diplomacy, but sometimes it is appropriate to say what you really feel and think and to assert your rights by directing your reactions where they belong, rather than burying them inside.

So, there are two kinds of stress, the usual stresses and strains of everyday life where you cope, but also distress where you begin to feel increasingly anxious, and acute distress can be triggered by a traumatic event.

What is a traumatic event?

'Post-Trauma Stress' refers to the stress, or rather, the distress you experience when you have been involved in a traumatic incident. But what is a traumatic incident? Let's begin at the beginning. Forget about major incidents for the moment and ask yourself:

- 'What was my first experience of trauma?'
- Pause . . . close your eyes and think about this before reading on.

What did you recall? Perhaps you remembered something that happened when you were young or the time when you were mugged, assaulted or verbally abused? Was it when your pet died, when you were bullied at school or work, rejected in love, in a car crash, experiencing a harrowing divorce or the death of a parent or other family member? The answer to the question could be 'When I was born', because this was a very stressful and traumatic occasion for both you and your mother. Joy that a child is born, yes, but also painful. Then, as you grow, you face further difficult experiences. You learn to relate to your mother and she and you are the whole world, but you slowly become aware of others around you demanding your attention: a father, brothers and sisters, in an ever-widening circle of family, friends and strangers. Gradually you learn to crawl and walk and begin to explore a fascinating and sometimes frightening world, and if you become anxious or think you are in danger you can crawl or run back to your mother for safety. Then, one day you are taken to school where you have to learn to relate to a large group of other children. Most can't remember it, but some adults recall this experience vividly and say that it was a very traumatic and painful period of their lives. Then, as you grow and develop, you move through a series of natural experiences: changing schools, puberty, leaving school and either going to college or university or looking for a job. During this time you have learned about making and breaking relationships and the pain they can bring. You might even have fallen in love and married, or moved into a

4

serious relationship or series of relationships, and have children, or you remain single. Gradually you grow older, your children leave home, you retire from work, your hair grows thin, or not at all, and you might have problems with hearing and mobility. Old age comes along and eventually you have to face the loss of a partner and your own death. This is the natural cycle of life: it involves a whole series of changes, losses and challenges, and these can be traumatic. As you grow, you change. You usually cope and adapt to whatever is new, sometimes not very successfully, but it is a progression of:

Growth → Change → Loss → Adapting → Coping

Growth brings change, change results in loss and you have to adapt in order to cope. Like stress, loss is part of growing and can be good or bad. Getting married or moving into a close relationship is a loss of your single status, but, hopefully, a good loss. Giving birth can bring great happiness and joy, but it is the loss of having the baby in your womb and a loss of some freedom because you have another human being to consider. Going through puberty is the loss of being a child, but means becoming an adult. You are changing from moment to moment until the day you die: you are not the same person you were when you started reading this book! Every growth brings change, so loss is a natural and normal human life-experience, but it sometimes results in painful reactions. It might be loss and change due to some single event, like being made redundant, or experienced over a long period of time. A difficult childhood with an uncaring and unloving parent can be devastating and may mean that later in life you might have difficulty in both giving and receiving love and in forming and maintaining loving and stable relationships. In a family where anger is never addressed or expressed other than to say, 'We never get angry in our family,' you might develop problems in coping with both your own anger and the anger of others. But whatever the traumatic incident, whether momentary or extended, a similar pattern of reactions emerges, typified by the 'SAD', Shock, Anger, Depression model often used to describe grieving. The change and loss result in *shock* followed at some stage by a host of different feelings, typified by *anger*. These feelings and emotions can be expressed or buried away and, if they are particularly painful and difficult, lead to sadness and *depression*. Life is a succession of changes and losses, good and bad, some of which are traumatic because they result in painful reactions.

One definition of Post-Trauma Stress is:

The development of characteristic symptoms following a psychologically distressing event outside the range of normal human experience.

The reactions are identifiable as similar responses common to many different, distressing situations, especially when the incident is beyond your normal experience. Seeing a mangled and burned body, being raped or mugged, being in a train or air crash or major disaster are not normal experiences for most of us, and you would expect them to be extremely disturbing. A police, fire or ambulance officer might experience some of these on a number of occasions and say, 'It's just part of the job. You just learn to live with it.' Professionals develop strategies for coping, but they are not insensitive to feelings or immune from developing quite severe reactions. They too can break down. Not everyone will experience the same reactions, but any reactions, to quote another definition, should be seen as:

The normal reactions of normal people to abnormal events.

But both of the above definitions raise similar questions. What are normal reactions? What is a normal person? What is an abnormal event? If you were extremely disturbed by something you had experienced and someone said, 'Don't worry, your reactions are normal,' you might reply very angrily, 'They don't feel normal, they feel dreadful.' The word 'natural' might be better: that these are your natural responses, but they might not feel natural. Similarly, what is an abnormal experience? If you are a nurse, holding a dying patient in your arms might be normal, but it can still be extremely distressing, no matter how many deaths you have experienced before. The balloon can only take so much pressure before it bursts. But are all your reactions normal? It would be normal to respond angrily if someone annoyed or upset you. It would not be normal if you murdered them. The problem is that whether you have experienced them before or not, and no matter how well trained or prepared you are, sometimes some experiences are overwhelming.

The argument so far is that life involves a series of events which result in various levels of stress and distress. Some are more painful and distressing than others and some devastate your life. In addition to these expected life-events there are other experiences which are also traumatic and which you would expect to be particularly distressing and disturbing. These 'major incidents' are:

- fatal accidents of all kinds, rail, road and air crashes and disasters at sea;
- natural and man-made disasters;
- war and combat experience;
- poverty, famine and disease;
- serious accidents of all kinds;
- shootings, bombings and terrorist activity;
- being held hostage;
- muggings, being beaten up, assaults and other experiences of violence;
- rape or sexual, physical and emotional abuse, either for a child or an adult;
- bullying of any kind – at school, work or in the home;
- armed robberies;
- being threatened, tortured and intimidated;
- witnessing serious incidents and seeing mutilated and dead bodies;
- riots and civil disturbances;
- difficult and distressing aid-agency work overseas;
- miscarriages, stillbirths, abortions;
- bereavement.

Until recently, miscarriage, stillbirth and abortion were not considered to be 'major' events, but it is now generally acknowledged that some people experience severe or chronic reactions.

In addition, there are other events which can be devastating for those involved:

- marital distress, separation and divorce;
- discovering that you were adopted;
- having your home broken into and being burgled;
- being made redundant;
- being bitten or attacked by an animal;
- being given bad news of a death, serious disease or terminal illness;
- disputes and arguments with other people, especially if bitter, on-going or long-term or if they involve anger or violence;
- being imprisoned.

Some people will accept these with stoicism while others find their lives almost destroyed. Separation, divorce and abortion happen so often that some would claim they are therefore normal and should not be too distressing! You might be relieved that a destructive relationship is over and just get on with your life, but this is far from the case for others. Even when you want a separation or divorce, you can still experience feelings of anger, guilt, blame, self-doubt, loneliness, rejection and failure, and the involvement of children can further intensify reactions. For some people, these events are major because similar experiences can be different for different people and not every incident is alike. I might be in a car crash and you are involved in a similar accident, but even if we are in the same car our reactions can be very different. Redundancy can be a shattering experience, even though it is relatively common, but can result in typical reactions to change and loss: shock, anger, feelings of rejection, a sense of failure and deep depression. Others might see such incidents as rather trivial: 'These things happen, but you just have to get on with your life and make the best of it.' To act otherwise would be seen as a sign of weakness or a 'lack of moral fibre', as was said of emotionally exhausted air-crew in the Second World War. The point is:

'If it is distressing for me, then don't tell me it shouldn't be or that it isn't. Whether or not you or anybody else coped, or could have coped, is meaningless, because you are not me.'

What is a traumatic incident? The answer is, whatever you find distressing. It could be a fairly minor incident, causing mild upset and distress which soon subside and you move on. It could be a major disaster, which devastates your life and the lives of many others. However, in spite of their experiences, some will deny that stress and trauma exist.

A retired police officer, all six feet four inches of him, attended a seminar on stress and trauma. Over coffee he said that there was no such thing as stress and trauma, because in his thirty years as a police officer he had experienced almost every kind of nasty event you could think of and these had never affected him one bit. He was asked how he had coped with particularly difficult incidents, and he replied that sometimes he could not sleep and would have many fitful nights. 'What did you do when you couldn't sleep?' he was asked, and he said, 'Oh! Often I would talk to my wife until two or three o'clock in the morning.' Someone asked him, 'Who did your wife talk to?'

Post-Trauma Stress is the physical and emotional reaction to being involved in a distressing event where your normal mechanisms for coping and adapting are challenged and might break down. Usually, reactions gradually diminish, but if they persist and intensify, you experience more and more difficulty in coping. You can cope better if you understand how you were involved, how you have reacted and why.

2
Who is Involved?

Who is involved? Just about everybody, because we all experience minor, and sometimes major, traumas throughout our lives, even if at different levels and with differing reactions. There are four main groups:

- the immediate victims;
- partners, families and friends;
- rescuers, helpers and other professionals;
- those with a general interest in trauma.

The immediate victims

Traumatic events of all kinds include people who are 'immediate victims' because they are at the centre of the incident. Even if surrounded by others, you can still feel that you are on your own and that nobody understands, perhaps not even those who were with you. You are a victim because it has happened to you.

Scene one
You are walking home late one evening on your own. It's dark in the street and you are anxious and hurrying because you told your partner you wouldn't be late. Suddenly a figure leaps out in front of you brandishing a knife and tells you to hand over everything you have on you of value. You are not Bruce Lee or Arnold Schwarzenegger so you do as requested, the mugger pushes you roughly to the ground and runs away.

Scene two
You have travelled to work on the same train every day without mishap. One day you are sitting relaxing when there is a sudden, violent crunch, a screeching of brakes followed by the sound of someone screaming and shouting. You wonder where the voice is coming from and discover, with shock, that it is coming from you and that you are injured and trapped.

Scene three
You are with your partner in the specialist's consulting room having had extensive X-rays and investigations when you realize that the consultant is speaking to you and telling you that you have cancer. You can't believe you are hearing it and suddenly feel numb. It's as though you have left your body and are looking down on someone else. What has he said? What does it mean? How will you cope?

In the first scene you are alone and mugged. In the second, you are with many other people, perhaps even people you know or recognize every day. In the third, you are with someone you love who shares the experience. Even when other people are present, you can still feel alone and isolated and that you are a victim.

You might be unhappy about being called, or labelled, a 'victim', or even of using the world to describe others. The word 'victim' can suggest someone who is helpless, hopeless and picked on: a Jonah, a jinx. Sometimes the situation is one which makes you helpless, hopeless and you are being picked on, and even if you aren't, this is how it feels. When someone points a gun at you, it is reasonable to assume that you could be killed. The gun might not be loaded, but you have no way of telling, so, because of what could happen, you do as you are told. To assume that the gun is not loaded would be stupid and illogical, so you do nothing. Sensible under the circumstances, but you can still think, 'I could have, should have, maybe, perhaps!' Similarly, you might feel guilty and that something is your fault, when, to others, it clearly isn't. You ask, 'How could God let this happen?' when you don't even believe in God. But that's how it feels. You feel helpless, hopeless, useless, weak, pathetic, picked on, guilty, angry and frustrated. You are a victim. But you could look at your experience and at yourself in a different way. What do you think of this statement?

You just happened to be there when something awful occurred.

How does this feel? Remember, you didn't ask to be a victim, but became a victim because of what someone did to you or because you were there at the time. Sometimes the situation is the result of what you have done, and if you have made a mistake you need to face this, but even when it's not your fault you can still feel that it is. If

11

only you could turn the clock back, change the past and make it different! 'If only I had been a few minutes earlier or later, I wouldn't have been involved.' 'If only I had been able to swim, I could have saved his life.'

'I am overwhelmed by these terrible feelings of guilt and anger. I don't know what's happening to me and nobody, not even my partner, seems to understand. What can I do to help myself and take me back to where I was before this happened?'

Well, you can't go back, but you can go forward. Believe it. There are ways through. You can help yourself, and others can understand, and how you think of yourself is important.

A man who had been viciously assaulted said, 'I eventually stopped thinking of myself as a victim, because that was negative. I'm not a victim. I'm going to think of myself as a *survivor*.'

It doesn't help everyone, and it doesn't wave a magic wand, but it might be a start to tell yourself that in spite of how you feel, you didn't ask to be a victim, and to remember that you have survived.

Partners and families
(See also pages 52–5 and Chapter 7.)

Perhaps you live or work with someone who has been in a traumatic incident? If you do, then this will almost certainly affect you and your family.

'He's in a bad mood today. Don't go near him.'
'I don't know what's got into him. He just keeps bursting into tears for no reason.'
'That accident seems to have pushed him over the edge. He's changed.'
'He's not the same person since he came home from . . .'
'I don't know what to do. I'm at my wit's end with him. He just won't talk to me and he hides in his own little shell.'
'He never shows me or the children any affection. I don't understand it.'

'He wakes up most nights shouting out and in a sweat. What should I do?'

'I just can't put up with it. I've had enough, and so have the children.'

'He never stops talking about it. He goes on and on until I could scream.'

You don't mind the occasional 'war story', but not minute after minute, hour after hour and day after day! But it is difficult to know what to do and say. How do you react to someone you love who is withdrawn and hardly ever speaks, who has bouts of irrational anger and tears and wants to be alone or wishes to cling to you like a baby, who has nightmares and wakes up sweating and shaking?

Also, if you were involved in the same incident, or one like it, you might think that because you have coped and it hasn't affected you, except for some initial shakiness, your partner should also be coping. Similarly, even if you have been affected, don't think that others should have reacted in the same way.

An army officer, who, as a young soldier, was one of a group of people clearing up body parts following a bombing, said, 'I remember shovelling bits and pieces into plastic bags, but since then, over twenty years ago, I have never thought about it or lost a night's sleep. I know that others were badly affected by it but I cannot understand why. Is there anything wrong with me for not reacting?'

But he had reacted, and his reaction, whether consciously or unconsciously, had been not to think about it or be disturbed by it. To suggest that he should have been affected badly would have been wrong. He reacted in a way which helped him to cope at the time and afterwards. But because he had coped well, it doesn't mean that his colleagues should have done the same. You will certainly not help others by telling them that you coped and by expecting them to be like you. We all have differences: different ways of reacting, different methods of adapting, different coping mechanisms and different ways of surviving.

After a serious traffic accident, a husband coped by hiding and controlling his emotions. His wife coped by crying and showing

13

emotional distress. Neither understood the other: he was accused of insensitivity and not caring and she of being too emotional. But both were coping in the way they knew best. After some months the man began to express his feelings and emotions, by which time she had stopped crying and wondered what was wrong with him!

Recognize the differences and respect them. Even if you were not directly involved in the incident you need to understand what has happened to your partner and also to realize that you will be affected. Sometimes hidden reactions can lurk around inside for years and then, for whatever reasons, begin to emerge. When this happens, you as a partner might have to take action.

A fire officer who experienced many traumatic situations, including a major disaster, coped well until his retirement. Four years after retiring, he began to experience bouts of anger and despair, nightmares and flash-backs. His wife thought that he was going mad; she found it increasingly difficult to cope with him and their relationship began to disintegrate. His reactions intensified and, in desperation, she persuaded him to consult a counsellor. Much against his will, but with her encouragement and support and a little bit of pushing, he eventually went for help.

If you live or work with a 'survivor', you need to accept the reactions as real and genuine, understand what the reactions have been and why, and try to respond in ways which are helpful and positive. Do not try to 'bolster them up' or 'jolly them along'. These suggestions don't usually work and might be interpreted as patronizing and as evidence of insensitivity and a lack of caring or understanding. Also, you need to understand that even if you were not involved in the incident you will probably be affected. You can't live with a depressive without being influenced in some ways, and the same is true if you live and work with survivors of traumatic events. Research tells us that even the grandchildren of those who survived the Nazi concentration camps can develop severe symptoms of Post-Trauma Stress just from living with them and hearing the stories and seeing the reactions, over and over again. Think how children might feel or react when their father is sometimes angry and violent or is withdrawn and doesn't want to play with them or speak to them. It's not just, 'What's wrong with Daddy (or Mummy)?' but, 'What's wrong with me that he doesn't want to be with me or to love me? What have I done?' There can be powerful feelings of rejection and self-blame in children as well as in adults. If this includes you, there are things you can do and say which will be helpful, and you can begin by trying to understand what has happened and how it has affected everyone involved, including you. These are discussed in Chapters 7 and 8.

Rescuers and helpers – the professionals

Because of your work you might come across trauma on a regular basis, sometimes every day. If you are a fire, ambulance or police officer, you can experience traumatic events, either through personal assaults or by attending incidents such as major disasters, traffic or other accidents, deaths, murders, fires, suicides, violent domestic incidents, rapes and sexual abuse cases. These can also be experienced by doctors, nurses, social workers, educational psychologists, prison officers, welfare and occupational health personnel and clergy, counsellors and workers with organizations such as Relate, Cruse, Victim Support and the Samaritans, mental health professionals, those involved with the unemployed and homeless, workers with drug addicts and those on probation, teachers, charity and overseas aid-agency workers, shop assistants, bank and building society staff and anyone responsible for goods or money. It also includes armed forces personnel who experience combat, threat, violence, being shot at or bombed, and even 'peace-keeping', where they can experience incidents which result in frustration and the impotence of being unable to do the job for which they were trained. This list includes just about everybody except hermits! All of these, and many more, can be immediate victims because they are at the centre of the incident.

They can also be 'secondary victims'. A secondary victim is someone who is not directly involved in the incident but is nevertheless affected by it, like the grandchildren of Holocaust victims mentioned earlier, or the partner of someone raped, assaulted or involved in a terrifying or horrific event. A police officer attending a fatal road accident can be traumatized by the experience and either be an immediate victim, as the driver of one of the cars in the incident, or become a secondary victim by attending the scene. A teacher can be seriously affected by the death of a child in school, or traumatized by being assaulted by a parent or pupil. Aid-workers overseas can be secondary victims through working with and seeing starving people and refugees, those who have been mutilated or tortured and dead bodies. But they can also be immediate victims through being assaulted, kidnapped, held hostage, raped or threatened or through the cumulative effects of their work.

Rescuers and professional helpers can also experience symptoms and reactions of Post-Trauma Stress. Many organizations, including the emergency services, now have strategies for helping people to cope with trauma through education and training and by using techniques such as Defusing and Debriefing, monitoring and supporting personnel, and offering support and counselling. These will be discussed in Chapter 8.

The general enquirer

Have you witnessed a traumatic incident? Are you a non-professional helper, a team leader, manager or supervisor, a colleague or even a member of a family where someone has been traumatized? You might even be a secondary victim! Perhaps you just have a healthy interest in learning about stress and trauma and how people might react and be affected? You hear about trauma every day in the media, wonder how on earth people are coping, and are sometimes angered by the insensitive reactions of others. You read in the papers or hear someone say:

> 'Emergency services are attending a fire in a house in Bradford where a four-year-old child was burnt to death. The parents were not available to comment and are still trying to come to terms with the tragedy.'

'Trying to come to terms with the tragedy'? They will probably still be trying in fifty years' time! This kind of statement shows how little some people understand or respect the reactions of others. When you watch scenes of major disasters on the TV, you might ask, 'Why do these things happen? Life seems so unfair. How on earth will people

16

cope and what can be done to help?' Some watch and listen to survivors and rescuers with compassion and horror: others come to the conclusion that these people are over-reacting and are weak or inadequate. Unfortunately this last view is common in society. 'Fancy a police officer breaking down and crying! Professionals should be able to cope and not get upset, no matter what happens.' Common remarks are:

'You knew what you were letting yourself in for when you joined.'
'If you can't take it, you shouldn't be in the service.'
'If you can't take a joke, you shouldn't have joined!'

But are these very realistic? Can you ever really know what you are 'letting yourself in for' when you undertake to do something? You can have some idea, and your training will help, but it's not the same as the real thing. How can you prepare a soldier for the experience of killing someone with a bayonet or having his mate shot dead beside him? You can teach him to bayonet a bag of straw, but a bag of straw is not the same as a living, breathing human being. Would you shoot his friend dead at his side so that he could know what it is like and you can see how he will react, and whether or not he will cope? I think not.

During a seminar on stress and trauma, a fire officer introduced himself by saying that he had recently gone through a painful divorce. When discussing the problems of stress and trauma, he said that as a fire officer, you 'knew what you were letting yourself in for when you joined so you shouldn't suffer in any way.' One of his colleagues suggested, 'You shouldn't have got divorced and you shouldn't have found it painful when you did, because you knew what you were letting yourself in for when you got married.' The fire officer thought about this for a few seconds and then replied, 'Point taken!'

Some people should never be emergency services' professionals, soldiers, nurses or doctors, and a selection process can help to exclude those who might be unsuitable. The real problem is this:

It is impossible to say exactly how anyone will react to an

incident, no matter how experienced, how well trained or supported, or how tough and resilient they might appear to be or think they are.

You don't always react to the same situations in the same ways, partly because there is no such thing as 'the same situation'. Similar? Maybe! Identical? No!

Because they are part of our human experience, information and knowledge about stress and trauma are essential elements in everyone's eduction. Knowing what you might experience, how you might react and what is available to help you can lead to reassurance and understanding. But what about 'the good old British stiff upper lip'? This will see you through anything. An attitude of gritting your teeth and bearing stoically whatever life brings along can help some people some of the time, but it doesn't help everyone all of the time. And if you keep a stiff upper lip, you can't speak properly and others won't understand you! But some still believe that reactions should not happen and that educating anyone about stress and traumatic reactions is wrong.

> A senior officer in the army said to the Debriefing group leader when they were about to Debrief people who had been held hostage, 'Aren't you trying to persuade these people that they owe themselves a problem?'

The officer seemed to believe that asking people about what they had experienced and offering information was putting ideas into their minds. 'Irritability and nightmares? I haven't had those yet. I think I'll have them tomorrow!' Similarly, the beliefs and attitude of a senior officer in the emergency services can be summed up by his comments:

> 'We in the West are becoming soft and not like the refugees and starving in the Third World. They just accept life as it comes and get on with it. If a woman has twelve children and ten die, then that's normal for her and it doesn't affect her one bit. You can see this on the faces of the starving women on TV. They just get on with their lives without moaning or complaining.'

I'll bet they do! Isn't it more likely that they have reached the point where there is no longer any hope or help and they are in a state of permanent shock and utter despair? Some even believe that if police officers, soldiers or other professionals are to be involved in seeing dead bodies, or experiencing war or a disaster, then you must not tell them that they might be frightened or horrified. 'If you tell them that they might be frightened, then they will be. If you don't tell them, they won't.' It makes it worse when people who believe this are in positions of authority and leadership, because it radiates from them and permeates and infects the whole system to which they belong. You might believe this from ignorance or because of the desire to appear hard and tough. It can also be anxiety and concern about your own ability to cope, and fear that showing compassion might be interpreted as a sign of weakness and others might not cope. Even John Wayne was afraid before he hit the beaches at Bataan! 'Gee, Major, I'm scared!' said a young private soldier in the landing-craft. 'So am I, son. So am I,' came the comforting reply!

Knowledge about trauma and the ways in which some might react or be affected can help, but some don't seem to want to know. How many people suffer from bullying and abuse of all kinds at home, at school or in work and never receive any help, understanding or compassion? How would you react if any of these happened to you or if you were involved in an accident or disaster? Would you, or others around you, especially those you love or work with, understand your reactions and feelings, and would they be supportive? Would they do and say helpful things? I have been involved in helping others after traumatic experiences for forty years, but I still don't know how I would react if any of these things happened to me. I just don't know how, or even if, I would cope, but I hope that knowledge and experience would help me, and that I would receive understanding and help from others and that they would not accuse me of being weak. Training, knowledge and information can help you to understand about possible reactions and to know what to say and do when disaster happens to you or to someone else. Ignorance can lead to stigmatizing others and labelling them as pathetic or inadequate, and this belief and attitude can persist in society, in organizations, in families and in individuals. You will probably cope better if you know how you might react or how you and others can be affected. Obviously, it depends upon how you are informed and what you are told, but information, given in the right way, can be reassuring.

It would be a better world, we would be better people and our relationships and lives would be better if we used our knowledge and experience to create a community and society where any reactions to stress and trauma were seen as natural and normal and not signs of weakness or inadequacy.

3

Understanding Physical Reactions

Perhaps you have been in a traumatic incident? You know how you reacted and you can clearly remember it now. Maybe you haven't, but wonder how you would react if something awful did happen to you. Would you just accept it, then forget it and get on with your life, or would you find it difficult and disturbing? 'Well,' you say, 'It depends on the incident!' Perhaps you think you would be weak or pathetic if you were very distressed and reacted badly, or that you are weak now because you don't think you coped well? Are you concerned about the reactions of others towards you who seem to say, 'I don't know what's wrong with you. You should be all right and coping instead of being like this'?

Scene 1
You have just been to the cinema and returned home with your partner. It was an exciting film and you enjoyed it, so you are both feeling quite elated. You put the key in the lock, open the door and walk in. There facing you is a scene of utter chaos. You have been burgled. The TV, video and some precious ornaments have gone and every chair, piece of furniture, picture and mirror in the room is smashed. Photograph albums have been scattered about and many of the photos, along with your favourite books, torn to pieces. Every room in the house is similar. For a moment you say nothing, then turn to your partner and say, 'Well, never mind. Lots of people get burgled these days and in any case it was only property. It's a good thing we weren't here when it happened. Let's get busy clearing up and go to bed. We can contact the police and insurance company in the morning.' You are perfectly calm and not in the least upset.

Scene 2
You are on your way to work in the car, driving down the motorway on a wet, icy morning. The traffic is building up and, as usual, most are driving too fast and some cars are even sliding and veering across the road on the ice. Because of the danger, you begin to slow down. A car overtakes you, crashes into the safety-barrier and a massive pile-up occurs with the noise of tyres

screeching and the smashing and crunching of car into car. You are trapped by the steering-wheel in the midst of a heap of tangled metal, but, as far as you can tell, not injured. You hear the screams and shouts of other people and the crackling of the engine. There is a strong smell of petrol, but you can't move. The thought enters your head, 'If I don't get out of here this is going to go up like a bomb and I'll be burned to death,' so you say to yourself, 'Well, there's nothing I can do, so I'll just remain calm and wait until the police and ambulances arrive.' You pick up a book from the passenger seat and sit and wait patiently, the petrol fumes swirling all around you and the hot engine tick-ticking away. Eventually you are rescued amid many mangled bodies and screaming injured. You even notice that some have been burned to death. After a quick check-up at the hospital, where they discover that you have a fractured bone in your arm and patch you up, you assure them that you are all right, go on to work and then home in the evening. What a busy and hectic day! You are all right, it hasn't affected you one bit and, that night, you sleep like a log.

Not very likely! Most of us would experience very different reactions. When you are involved in an incident, you are usually shocked, stunned and frightened, and not likely to have much control over your reactions. Your mind and body respond almost immediately with a battery of physical and emotional reactions which just surge up from inside and take over. How many times have you reacted strongly to a situation, perhaps of provocation or threat, and said afterwards, 'It wasn't like me to say and do something like that. I was so angry that I exploded with rage. I just don't know what got into me'? The point is, it was exactly like you: it wasn't anyone else but you! What got into you was you!

If you found your home broken into, you would almost certainly be shocked and stunned. At first you would find it difficult to believe that it had happened: you would be extremely angry and upset; your private space and world have been invaded; things precious and irreplaceable have gone or been destroyed; you feel vulnerable and that the place is no longer safe. You might feel cold inside and begin to shiver and shake or shout and cry. The odd swear word or two might come to your lips, with murderous feelings towards those who have done it, 'What I would do to them if I could get my hands on them!' It's doubtful if you would sleep well that night and the effects would probably be felt for some time. You might be reluctant to go out, and when you did, you might expect to return home to find that the house has been broken into again. There would be sadness and anger about the loss of precious articles and for the loss of security and safety. You might fit more locks on your windows and doors and even have a security alarm and closed-circuit television installed. Your home is no longer your castle!

The car crash would also generate strong reactions. You are already highly stressed before the car accident takes place, with the drive to and from work, often arriving home in a state of tension, angry and exasperated, complaining about the state of driving on the roads and blaming everyone from the drivers concerned to the police and government. This regular, high level of stress could make you either a careful and considerate driver or someone who should not be on the road! In this incident you become aware of what is happening, your muscles become tense and you clutch the steering wheel with white knuckles, desperately trying to steer a safe course and slow down, or unable to move because you are frozen with fear. When you realize you have survived, you feel a great sense of relief, immediately followed by fear at being trapped. The smell of petrol increases your terror and you struggle to escape, screaming and shouting for help, or you sit in a state of shock, convinced that you are about to die. The emergency services arrive and rescue you; although you are glad to be alive, your reactions are likely to be acute and it could take some time for you to recover.

After an accident, a man was trapped in his car and could smell petrol. He coped fairly well at the time, but later told his family and friends that he was terrified and thought he was going to be burned to death. He was jumpy and shaken and in a constant state of high tension and fear, expecting something to happen at any moment. A few days later he felt much better so took his wife's car to a petrol station and began to fill up with fuel. As the petrol left the nozzle, the fumes hit him and he dropped the hose, screaming out loud. He was sweating and shaking with fear and someone nearby had to put the petrol in for him. One year later, he still couldn't fill up his car with petrol because the smell left him panicking and frightened, with his heart pounding away in his chest.

Traumatic incidents will affect you, whether you want them to or not, but reactions can differ and are not always dramatic or explosive. You might not be unduly upset and find that you manage to cope fairly easily. You are annoyed and angry, but there is nothing you can do about it now, so you might as well get on with your life. Annoying and inconvenient, but not devastating. Sometimes you cope calmly at the time and react in other ways much later:

> The vicar called to tell a woman known to him that her husband had been killed in a car crash. She asked him in, he told her what had happened and she said, 'Oh, right. Would you like a cup of tea or coffee? Milk and sugar?' She remained in this state until she saw her husband's body.

Probably the initial shock protected her from accepting or believing something so terrible and enabled her to cope with the news. Denial is a powerful and usually a protective reaction to high levels of distress. You read earlier about the man who said he was not affected by clearing up dead bodies after a terrorist bombing. His defence and way of coping was to suppress his reactions and get on with the gruesome task. He was able to stay calm and get on with the job, and this was how he continued to cope. You do react to whatever is happening around you and even when you are calm, cool and in control these are your reactions. What happens later is another question.

But why do you react at all? To understand why and how you react to traumatic experiences, you need to look at what takes place in your brain and body. As you move from stress into distress, changes occur in your body and lead to what is known as 'the fight or flight syndrome'. Imagine you are a cave-man – or cave-woman!

> You are facing a tyrannosaurus. You have two choices: you can fight the dinosaur or run away. You could, of course, faint, lie down on the ground or run around screaming, but you are a cave-person so that wouldn't be right! Your brain sends out various messages to your body and your autonomic nervous system takes over. You don't ask for this to happen. It just does. Certain physical changes take place almost immediately, due to the release of hormones such as adrenaline, cortisol and noradrena-line into your system: your heart begins to beat faster and your

breathing increases. Blood drains away from the surface of your skin because it is needed elsewhere, so you look pale. The blood supply to your brain and muscles increases so that you can make decisions more easily and respond more quickly, and your mind becomes crystal clear. Glucose is pumped into your bloodstream, giving you extra energy, and your mouth is dry because your digestive system closes down. The main thing on your mind is survival. The release of many other hormones results in a high level of arousal and excitement and your body and mind are 'all hyped up and ready to go'. Your mind is alert, muscles are tensed and you can run faster and fight harder. All these physical and mental changes increase your chances of survival. Even though you might be frightened, fear can be a positive reaction and help you to fight even harder or run faster. You might begin to jump about and shout and scream in a release of tension, and this could frighten the dinosaur away. You probably don't stand much chance against a tyrannosaurus: but it wouldn't be there in the first place because dinosaurs were extinct millions of years before people emerged on the earth!

But the point is clear: when stress rises, certain physical and emotional reactions will automatically take place. Your brain is not only saying to you, 'Get ready! Look out for trouble!' but taking steps to help you to cope by altering what is happening through a massive release of hormones and chemicals into your brain and body. You will react physically and emotionally, whether or not you want to, and you cannot predict or guarantee exactly how you will react, when you will react or why. But these physical and emotional responses occur in order to help you to survive, sometimes at great expense to yourself or others, and there will be after-effects.

A woman in an air crash, with the aeroplane on fire, said that it was the fear and survival instinct which made her crawl over the tops of the seats, and even over other people, to get to an open window. She experienced deep feelings of guilt later over what she had done, but she survived when many others died.

Physical reactions

Physical and emotional reactions can occur before an incident begins, and the expectations of something happening can help you to prepare. Professionals find that their training and previous experiences usually enable them to cope. If a fire-fighter, on his way to 'a shout', hears that he is to attend a house fire in which there are fatalities, including children, this information will churn around in his brain and he will be thinking about any previous or similar incidents he has attended, what they were like, what he saw and did and how he reacted and coped. This previous experience doesn't mean that it will not affect him, but it can help him to prepare physically and emotionally. If it is his first experience of this kind, then he might be more anxious, more concerned about how he will cope and desperate not to let his colleagues down. On the other hand, an experienced officer, or a new recruit, might react by being very confident and yet be totally unprepared for what they have to face or with the way it affects them. These reactions before the incident will depend on many variable factors: training and preparation; expectations from your knowledge of the incident and your previous experiences; how long you have to prepare; your character and personality; your learned coping strategies; what other things are happening in your life. How your colleagues are reacting is also important. If they are anxious, worried and frightened, or calm, cool and confident, these can be infectious and you are likely to respond in similar ways.

The following list includes some of the many physical reactions you might experience. They can influence not only how you respond physically, but also your thoughts and feelings and the ways in which you interpret the experience. It does not include every possible reaction, or suggest that you should or will experience them all, but you will experience some of them at some level.

Shock

This is often the first response to difficult experiences and can result in utter astonishment and disbelief, with a numbing of emotions and feelings causing you to freeze so that you can't move. You might even be unable to speak. Your brain seems to be sending a message, 'The way to cope is not to believe it's happening, so switch off', and this initially helps you to cope. You are stunned for a while, but eventually other reactions emerge. If the physical shock causes a reduction in blood flow throughout your body then you might faint or collapse. Shock occasionally results in loss of memory or amnesia and sometimes a total denial that the incident has happened. You know that it has affected you, but still don't believe or accept that it has happened, especially if it is too painful and disturbing to recall, so your mind closes it off and buries it away. You might be able to remember some things from the incident, but not others.

Hysteria

A hysterical response can be anything from screaming, shouting or running around aimlessly in panic and confusion, to total numbness and collapsing in a faint. Some are unable to think straight, talk, walk or move.

Impulsive actions

You do and say things you wouldn't usually do, without thinking about or considering the consequences, and you can make wrong or inappropriate decisions. You might become violent and aggressive and hit out at somebody or something, or run away and hide. A frequent comment is, 'That's not like him. It's out of character.'

Listlessness

You become tired and exhausted and can experience chronic fatigue: you don't want to get out of bed in the morning and, when you do, you don't want to go to work, make any decisions or do anything. You are physically and emotionally drained and have a constant desire to sleep or rest. This can also lead to feeling that everything is pointless and meaningless.

Increased physical sensitivity and irritability

Noises, people and sensory experiences irritate you. What others do or say at work or at home can annoy you, and if people try to hug you or touch you, you push them away. The noise of your children playing can be unbearable, so you shout and get angry, telling them to stop, and you leave the room or the house to escape. Someone speaks to you and you take it the wrong way and either become angry and aggressive or cry and run away. 'My nerves are jangling and on edge all of the time and the least little thing irritates and upsets me.'

Exaggerated startle-response

Someone comes up behind you and touches you on the shoulder to attract your attention, and your reactions are out of all proportion.

Instead of turning around saying that you were startled, you respond with anger and aggression, even to the point of violence. You are 'jumpy' and agitated by things which impact on your senses, and a sight, sound, smell, taste or touch can result in a sudden 'knee-jerk' reaction. Seeing, hearing or smelling something which reminds you of the event can cause you to physically and emotionally jump with fear and shock (see page 23).

Pains or tightness in the chest

A tightness in the chest is common and this, with your heart pounding away, can make you think that you are about to have a heart attack, further increasing your fear and the feeling of panic or dread.

Increase in breathing rate

A natural reaction to distress is a fast heart rate, an increase in tension and a need for more oxygen, so you breathe faster. If this breathing rate continues to increase, you might begin to hyperventilate. You feel panic and fear and you can faint or believe that you can't breathe. Hyperventilation, closely related to strong feelings of anxiety, results in a lack of carbon dioxide in your blood. Your fingers and toes tingle and feel numb and you might even have twitches in your muscles. A common remedy is to increase the amount of carbon dioxide in your blood by breathing into a paper bag.

Fast heart-beat and palpitations

Your heart beats faster because of your body's need for more oxygen. You feel it thumping and hear it beating in your chest and this increases your belief and fear that there is something seriously wrong with you. In the American Civil War and the First World War, such reactions in soldiers were sometimes called 'soldiers' heart' in the belief that the heart was causing the problems. The fact that it was probably due to fear, anxiety and combat seems to have been ignored.

Sweating

If you are frightened and in a state of excitement with your heart pounding away, there is usually a need for your body to cool down, so you begin to sweat. This can further convince you that you are ill, and it can also be embarrassing because of the discomfort and increase in body-odour.

Physical pain

Even if you are not injured, you can experience pain in various parts of your body: stomach aches, headaches, and pain and tension in your chest, legs and arms. It can feel as though you have been punched hard in the chest or stomach. Bereaved people often say that the pain of grief is intensely physical: 'You feel empty. It's like being scraped out inside.' Others feel they have a lump in the throat, chest or stomach.

A dry mouth

This was mentioned earlier: you have a dry mouth because your digestive system closes down. The dryness results in a tightness in your throat and a constant need to swallow, so you become thirsty and need to drink. Sometimes there is a craving for food.

The desire to go to the toilet

You joke about this because fear can result in a loosening of various bodily functions, but it is distressing, uncomfortable and embarrassing, even when you know that it is a normal response to fear. If you wet or soil yourself, this makes it even worse, with increased feelings of shame and deep embarrassment.

Overconfidence

The adrenaline buzz can make you think and behave as though you are invincible and immortal. This can lead to acts of great courage and bravery, but also to some which are stupid and end in a catastrophe. Your body-language and bearing, as well as what you say and how you say it, exude a false confidence, and because you believe that what you are doing must be right you can make wrong decisions.

Calmness and acceptance

Being calm and accepting what is happening or has happened are physical responses as well as feelings. Some soldiers relate that it helps when you reach this stage because you accept that you could be killed and, instead of panicking and running away, a sense of peace and calm comes over you. You can still be afraid, but it doesn't overwhelm you. Being and staying calm can lead to sensible and carefully thought-out decisions and actions, which enhance your chances of survival. It can also mean that you don't even try to help yourself or others and you just sit or stand there, inactive and helpless.

Body-language, physical activity and movement

Before making a speech or going into danger, or when something happens suddenly and unexpectedly, it is natural to feel afraid or anxious. You begin to sweat and complain of 'butterflies in the stomach'. You pace around in an attempt to calm yourself down or you run around in a panic. You could have a pale, flat, dull, expressionless face, with arms and limbs slack, head down and shoulders slumped. You might be standing confidently, walking up and down, or shaking with fear, expectation or excitement. In situations of extreme threat, the physical response is often to curl into a ball, as though you want to be back in the safety of the womb.

Increased use of drugs

This is a common response to trauma and includes tobacco, alcohol and drugs, legal or illegal, often used in an attempt to dull the senses and diminish reactions: you smoke and drink more than usual. The reaction to shock or distress is often to offer whisky or brandy, 'Get it down you, it will do you good.' It can help, but alcohol is a depressant rather than a stimulant. It might help you to cope temporarily, but can lead to dependency, with negative, and sometimes disastrous, side-effects.

> After the Falklands War, an ex-soldier regularly smoked canna-bis, because he said that when he smoked it he felt great, even though he knew he would have to return to reality. He said, 'At least I feel good some of the time rather than bad all of the time.'

These are all physical reactions, but they obviously have emotional consequences, like the following.

Confusion

This can lead to an inability to think straight or make decisions, and you either sit motionless or wander around in a daze, gabbling or talking incessantly to yourself or to others. You might not know where you are, who you are or what you should do.

Silence, physical withdrawal and avoidance behaviour

You have a strong desire to be on your own, and you might withdraw physically and emotionally from people, places and situations. Someone described this as:

> The need to prevent others from asking you awkward questions which might resurrect painful and undesired memories of things you would rather forget.

You deliberately avoid people or situations and might become offensive and abusive, even to those you love, in an attempt to keep them away. You do not wish to talk about your experiences and become very angry and upset if asked or pressed to do so. You believe that your feelings and reactions are shameful and that others will not understand or will think you are pathetic and inadequate, so you draw away from them and feel more and more isolated. If you are difficult, hostile, angry or offensive with others, they will probably try to avoid you, and this vicious circle further increases your isolation and confirms the belief that there is something seriously wrong with you. You are convinced that even those who were with you don't understand, so you try to avoid them and any reminders. Some will avoid reunions, and even if they attend will not talk about the difficult things they have experienced. In spite of the horrors of war, the fiftieth anniversaries of the various events of the Second World War resulted in remembrance services and celebrations for many, but others found them too painful to contemplate and refused to take part in or attend social gatherings.

Obsession with the event

Unlike those who withdraw and wish to be silent about their experiences, you talk incessantly about the incident and how it has affected you, and this can be another cause of the isolation mentioned above. Nobody wants to talk to you, 'because he just goes on and on about it until I could scream!' Keeping detailed diaries and records, collecting and hoarding memorabilia, newspaper cuttings and photographs are not unusual. A combat veteran said, 'My war experience was the highlight of my whole life and everything before or since has paled into insignificance. That's why I need to talk about it and remember it.'

Restlessness and sleep disturbances

Some cannot sleep, while others find it difficult to stay awake. When asleep, dreams and nightmares occur, often of being in situations where you are not in control. A description of a recurring dream was, 'It's like trying to run through a field of treacle with something terrible and horrible chasing you and slowly catching up.' Possibly, these dreams represent how you felt during or after the incident and how you might feel now: something, or someone, has taken control over your life and you were, and still are, helpless. Some people wake up sweating, shaking and frightened, sometimes shouting out loud. If you are unable to sleep, you might pace around restlessly in a state of agitation, becoming increasingly anxious and distressed.

Physical violence against objects or people

Anger is a natural reaction to distressing situations, often accompanied by the desire to blame, take action and seek revenge. Sometimes it comes out in short sharp bursts and is directed against objects, other people or even against you. It can come out of the blue, apparently from nowhere, or it can be triggered by external events.

> A man, suffering from traumatic stress, came home to find that his wife had moved some furniture. His response was to punch his fist into a door and smash crockery. He revelled in venting his anger against waiters and traffic-wardens and enjoyed situations of high drama. He said, 'It's great to have the adrenaline rush. It makes me feel alive again.'

These are some of the many possible physical reactions, and they can be anything from mildly annoying or slightly upsetting to very disturbing and distressing. They are normal and natural reactions but, usually, even severe reactions gradually diminish as time passes. Don't automatically think there is something wrong with you if you experience them and do accept that physical reactions will also influence what you feel and think.

4

Understanding Emotional Reactions and Feelings

Emotional and physical reactions are not separate. If you are threatened, a normal emotional response is to be frightened, and the same threat which produces the fear causes your body to respond physically in ways which, hopefully, give you a better chance of coping and surviving. You might suppress the fear, and appear unconcerned and in control, but the fear is still there inside. 'I'm not angry or afraid' – but your body-language, the flashing, narrowed or staring eyes, the clenched teeth and fists and the way you speak, give another message. There is a theory, popular some years ago, that a bodily, physical posture can result in or cause emotional reactions. Try these:

Exercises

- Think of a time when you were really happy and laughed out loud. Smile as broadly as you can and adopt the appropriate bodily response. Hold the physical posture, the wide smile and sparkling eyes. Then, keeping your body in the same attitude, attempt to feel very sad at the same time.
- Imagine a time when you were extremely angry and felt as though you wanted to do something about it. Try to get in touch with that anger. Screw up your face, clench your teeth and fists and the muscles in your whole body in an attitude of fury and aggression. Hold it – then, keeping this posture, try to feel happy.

Even if you could do these exercises, you probably found that it wasn't easy. When you feel angry, you might try to stay relaxed and calm, but your natural physical reaction is to automatically adopt the appropriate bodily stance signifying anger and aggression to others. Your body-language signals, 'Beware! Keep away! I'm ready for you.' However, in the modern world you are expected to be 'civilized': be polite, never get angry, and if you do, don't show it. But these physical and emotional reactions happen, whether you want them to or not.

Let's suppose that you are feeling really angry at the way you have been treated. Your natural reaction is to express the anger or walk away, but you can do neither because you are in a car or restaurant or with your partner or boss. The hormones and feelings generated are surging away inside, but you grit your teeth, control yourself and push the feelings and energy down inside. But suppressing physical responses and emotions creates other reactions. Your mind begins to say, 'There must be something wrong with me. Why do I feel so angry and tense inside? I must be going mad.' One basic theme in this book is for you to repeat a mantra such as:

'There is nothing wrong with me except that I am in, or have been in, a situation which has caused me to react in this way. It was not of my choosing and it's not my fault that I'm like this. My reactions, even if distressing, are natural. Don't blame me, blame the incident or the person or people who caused it.'

Make up your own. Write it down on a card, carry it about with you and say it to yourself over and over again (see pages 60–1). It isn't an instant cure, but it can help you to keep things in perspective and restore the balance between what you have experienced and your reactions to it.

Traumatic events generate powerful emotions and feelings. The following reactions are typical and, like physical reactions, they can be mild and short-lived or severe and persistent. As with the physical reactions, you will notice similarities in reactions under the different emotions.

Anxiety

Anxiety can range from mild uneasiness to intense fear and dread, and can occur before an incident begins and still be present when it's over.

- 'Will I survive? Will I do my best or will I fail?'
- 'I'm not going to cope and I'll let others down.'
- 'I feel so anxious and wonder what's going to happen in the future.'

An increase in breathing rate and hyperventilation, muscle tension, an inability to relax or sleep and aches and pains in the body intensify the anxiety and can lead to feelings of depression, doom and despair. You think you have a serious illness or disease and believe that something awful is going to happen at any moment. You might feel depersonalized or experience 'out of body' sensations and believe that it is happening to someone else.

Vulnerability

When something awful or unexpected happens, your beliefs about yourself and the world are challenged. You feel angry, attacked, picked on and threatened. 'Why me? This shouldn't be happening.' Your sense of security and safety is shattered, and doom and disaster can dominate your thoughts and actions. Not only were you vulnerable then, you are vulnerable now. Anxiety, anger, fear and panic can follow (see pages 62–3).

Hyper-vigilance

Your mind and body are vividly alert: something has happened and it can happen again. Watch out! Life is no longer safe or secure: you are under threat. It's possible that you might learn something from the experience: you drive more carefully, at least for a few miles; for a while you avoid places and people likely to threaten you; you watch out for any signs of danger or threat, fit an alarm to your car or home and avoid doing anything risky. But this is not so for everyone.

Julie would walk down the street thinking, 'Something awful is going to happen to me before I get to that shop.' She would sweat and be in a state of tension and fear, looking around all the time in expectation. When she reached the shop and nothing had happened, she would sigh with relief, but then say, 'It's going to happen before I get to that next corner.' The pattern was repeated over and over again.

This reaction, like the 'exaggerated startle-response', (see pages 27–8), can result in a sudden physical jerk or jump in response to

35

anything unexpected. You react with aggression and violence or shake with fear.

Fear

Fear can generate emotional and physical energy which helps you to survive: you either fight or run away. It can also be disabling and petrifying, where you feel terrified and helpless. It can be translated into other areas of your life where you are frightened by the least thing and become anxious, agitated and nervous.

Panic

Panic is a physical reaction as well as a feeling and is a combination of fear and anxiety. You rush around aimlessly, sometimes shouting and screaming or talking without making sense. You do the wrong things or make inappropriate decisions because you are blind to further danger or threat. It can also be paralysing. The panic might enable you to run away and survive, provided you run fast enough and in the right direction!

Concern

This can either be selfishness and thinking about yourself or concern and caring for others. You make the right decisions and take appropriate action, like the woman who survived the plane crash by crawling over other people (see page 25). Concern for others takes your mind off your own feelings so that you are able to think straight, but if you are over-concerned, either with yourself or with others, the feeling instensifies and can lead to anxiety and indecision.

Confusion and uncertainty

'I feel stuck in a rut and don't know what to do. It's all so confusing.' You might be unable to make decisions and become silent and inactive or rush around shouting and screaming, not knowing who you are, where you are or what you should do.

Helplessness

If you are in a threatening situation, you might decide to do nothing, because whatever you do might have dire consequences and you, or others, might be injured or killed. You are helpless, but realize it is a conscious and sensible choice. But feeling helpless could be the result of acute fear, horror or dread. Either way it can lead to feelings of guilt and the belief that you should have been able to do something:

> A young man working in a building society faced an armed robber, had a shotgun thrust into his face and calmly gave him the money. Afterwards he was torn with feelings of helplessness and guilt and felt that he should have been able to grab the gun and overpower the robber. Being a body-builder made it worse. The fact that giving him the money was company policy, that the gun might have been loaded and that if he had tried to do anything, he, or someone else, could have been killed, didn't seem to matter. The feeling of helplessness was overwhelming, and it persisted and invaded other areas of his life so that he began to be fearful of doing anything which he saw as 'risky', even when it wasn't. Going back to his workplace was a nightmare, and when travelling on a bus or walking in the street, he expected to see the gunman again.

These reactions persisted for two weeks and, even though he recovered, he could still recall the feeling of being helpless. A sight, sound, touch, smell or taste can trigger the reaction.

> A woman who had been mugged went home and threw her husband's aftershave away because she said that it was the same as that used by her assailant and would remind her of him and trigger fear and helplessness. She laughed about it later because her husband's only comment was that the aftershave was expensive!

A sense of futility, pointlessness and disillusion

You begin to feel that what you are doing, or have done, is quite pointless. You are like an automaton or robot, performing purely because of your training or the need to get on with living. What you have seen and experienced is so overwhelming that everything is now trivial and unimportant.

A police officer who had attended a horrific traffic accident did not want to get out of bed in the morning. He saw no point in going to work, making decisions or in doing anything. He said, 'When you have experienced what I have been through, life, people and events seem shallow and insignificant. Why bother and why go on? Nothing matters any more.'

Anger, aggression and violence

You feel picked on and angry and need to blame someone or something. This can be anything from mild irritation to aggression and rage. 'Why has this happened and why me?' You can be angered by things that wouldn't normally upset you and direct this at anyone, especially your family, friends and colleagues, even at someone who is trying to help. You blame God, even if you have no religious beliefs, and, where someone has been injured or killed, you can even direct the anger and blame at them. The anger can erupt into violence, although this is usually directed at objects rather than people (see pages 32, 51 and 82).

Numbness of feelings

This usually comes with the initial shock, but can happen at a much later stage. You don't feel anything except physically and emotionally numb. Others speak to you or do things which would normally elicit a response, but you are unable to react. You feel nothing. This can be an extension of your body's coping mechanisms: you need to rest and have time to recover, so your emotional reactions close down; the experience is too painful so you protect yourself from your own feelings by shutting them off and by shutting out other people.

Euphoria and elation

It is natural to be elated and thankful when you have survived, but this can turn to disappointment and to feeling 'down' as the adrenaline boost wears off. It's the calm after the storm. Alternatively, to begin with you feel sad and disappointed, angry and

38

frightened, but as time passes this can lead to feeling a great sense of achievement. You are surprised at your own ability to cope and discover new self-esteem and self-confidence (see page 50).

Sadness and depression

When there is a sense of loss, sadness is a natural reaction and can lead to depression, but these two emotions are not the same. When you are sad, you usually feel alive, but when you are depressed you can feel nothing but a deadness inside: all seems to be hopeless and without meaning or purpose.

Intrusive thoughts and images

Thoughts and images just slide into your mind, usually when you don't want them to. These can either be triggered by some external event such as a sight, sound, smell, taste or touch which reminds you of the incident, or come 'out of the blue', when you aren't thinking about it, when you are reading, relaxing or thinking of something else. They might be mildly upsetting or come as vivid flash-backs, where you feel that the incident is happening again and you are devastated, terrified, frightened, sweating and shaking. Sometimes it's a picture where the image is clear: you see an object, a person or scene and this triggers disturbing memories. At other times it can be a thought or question: 'I should have been able to do more, but I was so helpless. I'm pathetic and useless.' 'Why didn't I do something?' Dreams and nightmares are also common intrusive reactions. The thoughts and images can also be positive and comforting.

Shame, remorse, bitterness, guilt and survivor-guilt

'Could or should I have done things differently?' 'Did I do enough?' 'Did I do the right things?' These thoughts can trigger feelings of shame, remorse, bitterness and guilt. For survivors of experiences where others have been injured or killed, 'survivor-guilt' is common. Instead of 'Thank God I am alive' you say, 'I should be dead. Others are dead, so why not me?' Both guilt and survivor-guilt can eat away inside, leaving you with feelings of deep sadness, regret, depression and disillusionment. If you were involved in an incident where you made a mistake, or caused it to happen, the guilt can be more severe and lead to physical or emotional withdrawal from your family or community, an inability to cope with work and, in a minority of cases, even self-harm or suicide.

Isolation and loneliness

Difficult experiences can set you apart from others: your partner, family and friends were not there so they don't understand. Alternatively, you only want to be with those who were involved with you, but even they might not know how you feel. Such feelings can lead to frustration, isolation and loneliness. Others feel threatened by you and fear that what has happened might be 'catching'! Initially you might not want to talk, so everyone assumes that you are all right, but four weeks later you need to talk. Because the incident was some time ago, others say, 'You haven't mentioned this before and, anyway, you should have got over it by now.' This not only increases the feeling of isolation, but drives you further away and intensifies your feelings of anger and hopelessness.

These reactions can influence what you believe and the way you think and, in turn, your beliefs and thoughts can affect how you react. This is explored in Chapter 5.

Post-Traumatic Stress Disorder

It is important to stress:

The above reactions, whether physical or emotional, are natural and usually temporary responses to traumatic events.

Thoughts and feelings keep coming into your mind, especially when something or someone reminds you and triggers the reactions. You experience them for a while, but they gradually diminish as time passes. They do not entirely disappear from your memory, and some can be recalled many years later, resurrecting some of the feelings and emotions you experienced at the time. But you cope.

There are some incidents and reactions to them which are not easily or comfortably recalled, and some will generate powerful and very disturbing emotions. If you were sexually or physically abused as a child, have lost someone you love or were in a devastating and horrific incident, you would not expect your memories of the experience, and your reactions to them, to be mild or easy. You want to forget, but no matter how hard you try, your life has been changed and the memories, physical reactions and emotions associated with the event come flooding back. But, even with severe reactions, you can look at how and why you have reacted and learn ways of adapting and coping. However, if the reactions and feelings persist and intensify, they can take on a very different nature in their effect and in their quantity and quality.

Following the Vietnam War, 15 per cent of veterans developed severely disturbing symptoms and reactions, both physical and emotional, and many found their relationships, health and ability to cope with life ruined. Some reactions were similar to those of people involved in civilian disasters, violence, rape and child sexual abuse. Eventually, in 1980, in a book produced by the American Psychiatric Association, known as the *DSM* (*Diagnostic and Statistical Manual of Mental Disorders*), these reactions, both to combat and civilian experiences, were placed under the umbrella of what was called, for the first time, 'Post-Traumatic Stress Disorder', or PTSD.

In the *DSM IV* (1994), the diagnostic criteria for PTSD are that the event is experienced, perceived or witnessed as a threat to life or of serious injury, there should be intense fear, helplessless and horror, plus elements of three basic reactions.

Re-experiencing

These are the 'intrusive' symptoms: recurrent and intense flash-backs with thoughts and images intruding into the present causing you to relive the experience; you have disturbing nightmares and dreams, usually waking up sweating and crying out; there is intense psychological and physiological distress at exposure to reminders of the event.

Avoidance behaviour – not present before the trauma

Avoidance reactions are: a numbing of feelings and emotions; efforts are made to avoid thoughts, feelings, conversations, activities, places or people that might or will arouse recollections of the event; an inability to recall memories of the trauma; a lack of any interest in taking part in family or social activities; feelings of detachment from others; an inability to express affection or love; a foreshortened sense of the future and feelings of doom and disaster.

Arousal symptoms – not present before the trauma

These reactions include: an inability to sleep; irritability and outbursts of anger or violence; difficulty in concentrating; hyper-vigilance and an exaggerated startle-response.

In addition, the reactions must cause severe disruption of the ability to cope with relationships, work and life in general. If the symptoms occur for less then three months, they are called 'acute', 'chronic' if they last for three months or more and 'delayed onset' when they appear more than six months after the incident. They can also be associated with a breakdown in health, severe depression, alcoholism and drug abuse. Within the first month following the incident, these symptoms would not be diagnosed as PTSD but usually referred to as Acute Stress Disorder (ASD), and they might or might not lead to the development of PTSD.

The problem with PTSD is that nobody knows what causes it, why it develops or who will experience the symptoms. It is not just an extension of Post-Trauma Stress with mild PTS at the lower end and PTSD at the higher end of a line of possible reactions. Also, it can develop not only after major disasters and war and combat experience, but also after apparently 'minor' events: traffic accidents, muggings, various medical procedures, operations, heart attacks, difficult childbirth and some of the many incidents mentioned in Chapter 1. It is possible, but far from certain, that the following factors might influence its development:

- the traumatic nature of the event;
- any preparedness and training;
- the nature and quality of support during and after the incident;
- vulnerability due to other factors: character and personality, previous or present difficult experiences and learned coping strategies;
- genetic factors.

But this does not mean that because you have experienced a highly traumatic event, are given no preparation, help or support during or after the incident, come from a difficult and disturbed background, seem previously to have coped badly with stress and trauma and have other serious problems in your life, that you will develop PTSD! Most people who develop early symptoms of PTSD recover within a few weeks. A tiny minority find that symptoms persist or intensify so that PTSD is diagnosed. In some cases, reactions do not occur immediately after the incident but lie dormant and emerge years later.

A police officer had experienced many traumatic incidents during his 30 years' service, but coped well. Four years after he retired, he began to have nightmares and flash-backs to certain events and he suffered severe bouts of anger, despair and depression. PTSD was diagnosed.

PTSD puts the sufferer into a different realm of experience and existence, and research suggests that there are significant changes in the workings of the brain. Research is being carried out into PTSD and the physiology of the brain and how it reacts to an increase in levels of stress and trauma, but there are no firm conclusions. What seems clear is that excessive levels of stress and trauma can result in alterations in the neurobiological processes within the brain and that these will influence ways of thinking and the beliefs held about self, others and the world. Most people will experience Post-Trauma Stress reactions at some level and recover: a minority will develop Post-Traumatic Stress Disorder. But it seems clear that Post-Traumatic Stress Disorder is not simply an extension of Post-Trauma Stress. Reactions can be similar, but are very different in effect.

In his book on severe depression, Lewis Wolpert calls it in the title, 'Malignant Sadness'. Perhaps PTSD is 'Malignant Distress', severe or chronic distress gone wrong? Professor Wolpert's book is worth reading, not only for what he has to say about depression, but because of his comments on and information about stress and PTSD.

If after reading this you think you might have PTSD, do not think that nothing can be done: *look for help*! You might find that you now have information which helps you to understand what is happening to you, but that you need much more. There are people who can understand and there is help available. You might not have PTSD, but severe or acute symptoms of PTS. Advice and suggestions for coping are given in Chapter 7 and more information about help in Chapter 8.

References

Diagnostic and Statistical Manual of Mental Disorders IV (DSM IV), American Psychiatric Association, Washington DC, 1994.

Wolpert, Lewis, *Malignant Sadness – The Anatomy of Depression*, Faber & Faber, London, 1999.

5

Living with Post-Trauma Stress

Have you experienced a traumatic incident? If so, it will affect you, your partner, children, friends and those you work with. If you live with someone who has been traumatized, you might not know what's happening or what you can do or say to help. Children will also experience the effects, either because they have been involved in an incident or because they live with someone who has. Like ripples from a stone thrown into a pond, the effects of trauma spread out, affecting an ever-widening circle of people. Even professional rescuers and helpers, who experience trauma on a regular basis, do not go unscathed.

The victim/survivor

Whether you see yourself as a victim or a survivor, remember:

You wouldn't have been affected if you hadn't been involved in a traumatic incident.

This is logical, but it might not feel like that and can be difficult to accept or believe. The experience can devastate your life and relationships and you wonder how you are going to cope. When you realize that it is also affecting your partner and children, it can tear you apart with feelings of guilt and helplessness. It can help you to understand what has happened to you if you realize that your reactions to the trauma will be influenced by a number of factors. Where there are questions, think about them and try to answer them. Writing down your answers can make them clearer in your mind.

The nature of the incident
- How horrific, threatening, terrifying and disturbing was it?
- Were you prepared, or was it sudden and unexpected?
- Did you think you might die? Could you have been killed or injured?
- Were there fatalities and injured, and did they include children or young people?

45

- Do you feel that the incident took control of your life away from you?

As a general rule, the more sudden, unexpected, traumatic and distressing the incident and the longer you are exposed to it, the more powerful your reactions will be. Believing that you are going to die is a devastating experience. The feelings can persist so that even thinking about it makes you afraid. Reactions can be more intense and disturbing when people are killed or injured, especially if children or young people are involved. Also, sensory impressions from the event can trigger frightening and horrible reminders.

A young police officer was called to a house where an old man had burned to death in bed. His cigarette had set fire to the bedclothes. Years later, as an Inspector, she said that she had never eaten roast pork since, because the smell brought back disturbing memories.

Loss of control

Loss of control is also an important factor. Usually you feel that you have some control over your life and you believe that bad things happen to other people (see invulnerability, pages 63–4). It couldn't happen to you! When you are involved in a traumatic event, you realize, unbelievably, that it can. Something, or someone, has taken control away from you. You feel helpless, vulnerable, confused, angry, afraid, threatened and a failure. You are weak and life is increasingly unpredictable. This is how you might feel, but remember the facts:

- it was the incident which triggered your reactions;
- the worse the incident, the more severe your reactions.

Your own experiences, past and present
(See also page 62.)

- What problems did you have in your life before the incident happened?
- Apart from the effects of the incident, have there been other difficulties since?
- How have these influenced your reactions?

- How vulnerable were you at the time?
- How vulnerable do you feel now?

'I've experienced these kinds of incidents before and I'm quite a tough character, so why was I affected so badly?' Reactions to a traumatic event can be exacerbated if you already have problems in your life: a relationship where you are angry and hurt; work is becoming increasingly difficult and stressful; you have on-going altercations with your neighbours; you are already disillusioned, depressed or ill. The cumulative effects of stress can mean that one further experience drives you over the top. It's the last straw! Life is difficult enough, but you are involved in a traffic accident, your son is mugged and beaten up, you are threatened with redundancy or your best friend dies. Usually you would cope calmly and sensibly, but you are so vulnerable that you over-react and feel that your life is falling apart.

Personal coping strategies

- How easily do you express your emotions?
- Did you suppress them and keep them under control? Why?
- Did you express them during or after the event? When, and in what ways?
- Were you able to do anything to help yourself or others?

The ways in which you coped will also determine how you reacted. You might use denial, control your feelings, remain calm and cool, react hysterically or become angry and aggressive. These are all possible ways of coping. Try to work out how you coped and why, what mechanisms you used for coping and how you are coping now. These can give you some idea of why you reacted as you did.

Training and preparation

- How prepared for the event were you?
- Did any previous experience or knowledge help you to cope? How?
- Given the incident, should you have reacted differently?
- Do you think of yourself as tough and resilient? If so, how tough are you?

If the incident just happened and you were not prepared or trained for it, then your reactions can be more intense. But being trained and prepared does not mean that you are invulnerable! A gradual build-up of stress can diminish anyone's ability to cope, and some experiences are overwhelming. Even experienced professionals can have problems.

Support

- Were you isolated and alone?
- If others were involved, how helpful and supportive were they, during and after the incident?
- How did your family and friends treat you when you went home?
- Was there intrusive and unsympathetic behaviour from the press or media?
- Did you receive any support or help when you returned to work?

If you were given little or no support during the incident, especially if you were on your own, and if others just expected you to 'get on with your life' when it was over, this can result in a deepening of guilt, confirmation of the belief that there must be something wrong with you and anger at their inability or unwillingness to understand. Intrusive behaviour by the media can also intensify your reactions.

Conclusions

If the incident was horrific and terrifying, if you have little or no preparation and training, if you are already vulnerable, if the support was poor or nonexistent, your ability to cope will be reduced. But, you can be tough, hard, well trained and ably supported and still develop severe reactions.

Other reactions

These reactions can apply to anyone involved in the incident.

Denial

Denial, a natural reaction to shock, gives you time and space to adjust and can help to protect you from reactions and feelings which might overwhelm you. You might even have difficulty in believing that the incident has happened! For professionals, this strategy helps them to cope with extremely distressing events and to get on with the job of saving lives. However, the continued use of denial can mean that you never face up to your true feelings. Hidden feelings don't go away.

Talking

You might not want to talk about the incident to anyone, your family included, because it would be too distressing, or you talk incessantly with such intensity and emotion that others either switch off or avoid you. Talking can help, especially to someone you trust. 'A problem shared is a problem halved!' But this is not true for all problems or for everyone.

Inability to show love or affection

- Are you able to express feelings towards those you love?
- Would expressing your emotions make you feel vulnerable and would others think you are weak?
- Do you feel a dullness and deadness inside?
- Do you feel unlovable and that nobody could love you?

Perhaps there is little or no warmth or comfort because you appear to have rejected those close to you and your reactions push them further away? This can affect your sex life, convince your partner that you don't love them and make you feel more useless and impotent. If you both feel isolated and alienated, even if you want closeness, warmth and sex, neither might be able to respond (see page 84). Because of the ways you have reacted, it is common to feel that nobody could love you.

Irritability, anxiety, difficulty in making decisions and loss of skills

Making decisions can be difficult. You feel under pressure and become increasingly anxious, irritable and confused. When anyone speaks to you, you misunderstand, and the normal hurly-burly of family life upsets and distresses you. You might even lose some mental, mechanical or physical skills for a while: driving, typing, spelling or operating a computer or machinery. This makes you feel even more incompetent and useless.

The desire for change

- Do you feel the need for changes in your life? What changes?
- Have your self-image and beliefs altered? If so, how and in what ways?
- Would changes be better? For whom and in what ways?

Trauma can result in dissatisfaction with almost every area of your life. As a general rule, it is usually unwise to make major decisions or changes soon after a traumatic experience.

Positive effects

Reactions are not all doom and gloom and there can be very positive effects:

- You discover a new meaning and purpose in life and have a deeper appreciation of life in general. The world seems a better place in which to live.
- You value relationships, partner and children, family, friends and work more.
- You are surprised at having coped and survived and your self-confidence increases.

These reactions can be due to post-survival euphoria, but experience suggests that they might not occur until much later. If your feelings are fairly negative, give yourself time.

Effects on relationships

If you are experiencing reactions to a traumatic event, you will probably find life difficult, you will be difficult to live with and relationship can become increasingly strained. You feel angry, afraid, irritable and unreasonable, and those around you don't seem to understand what you have been through or how you feel. Is it any wonder that you find it hard and that others don't know what to do to help you or how to cope?

The following can influence relationships.

Changes in beliefs
(See also pages 69–71.)

Your beliefs and faith, of whatever kind, can deepen and your self-image and confidence increase. It's good to be alive! Whether you believe in God or not, you might think that you have survived for some greater purpose and search for meaning and fulfilment. Some believe that their distress and suffering bring God nearer. Alternatively, you say there is no God or, if there is, he is cruel and remote. Fate has taken control of your life so you become either cynical and pessimistic or angry and furious. Life seems so unfair. Or you might accept what has happened and carry on, believing that this is your karma or destiny, and face it with resignation, courage and faith.

Silence, withdrawal and apathy

You feel unable to talk about what has happened and how you feel, and although your family want to know and understand, you retreat behind a wall of silence. It feels easier to be isolated so that you are not threatened, but it makes it extremely difficult for others. They try to understand, but might think that you don't care.

Obsession with the event

You might become obsessed with the event, constantly talking about it or about your feelings, and this can drive you and your family further apart (see page 31).

Dreams and nightmares

If you wake up in a sweat, perhaps frightened and shouting out, or twitch and jerk in bed and roll around restlessly, even though you are asleep, it is not only difficult for you, but also disturbing and upsetting for your partner and children. (See page 41.)

Anger

Even if it only emerges occasionally, anger will affect your whole family. You might control your feelings, but eventually you explode and vent your anger, smashing objects, driving dangerously, behaving unreasonably and objectionably at home, at work or in public. People treat you like a bomb with a short fuse (see pages 32, 38 and 82).

Effects on health

Changes taking place in your mind and body can affect your health (see pages 28–9). Emotional and physical reactions can result in headaches, stomach aches, pains and tension in various parts of your body, rashes and skin disorders, nausea and sickness, dyspepsia and ulcers. The feeling during an incident that you are about to die can make you think that you will die in the near future, so you must be seriously ill. These are known as 'psychosomatic' effects, the assumption being that worries, anxieties and difficult events can result in physical illness. You might become so obsessed with your health that, despite medical reassurance, you know that you are ill. Hypochondriacs are difficult to live with!

Partners

Living with someone who has been traumatized can affect you and your whole family. The first thing is to try to understand the reactions and what effects these have had on everyone.

Has your partner been involved in a traumatic incident? Seems like a silly question! However, it might be that you know that everything is not all right and that your partner has changed, but you have never connected this with anything that has happened in the past. If there has been a change in behaviour, whether gradual or sudden, ask yourself if your partner has been in a traumatic event.

A woman was concerned because her husband had changed in character. He was irritable when trivial things happened, easily lost his temper, became withdrawn emotionally, sometimes showed little affection or interest in her or the children and was drinking more than usual. Eventually she remembered that he had been in a train crash some months before, but thought that he had got over it because he never talked about it and seemed to have coped well. It transpired that he was now finding it difficult because reactions were emerging, many months later, and he was ashamed to talk about it or ask for help.

It might be nothing to do with trauma, but the result of something else that is happening in your partner's life. However, it is worth checking.

Physical and emotional withdrawal

If you know that something has happened to your partner and that something is wrong, no matter how hard you try you might be unable to get near. You are kept at a distance both physically and emotionally (see page 31).

A traumatized ex-serviceman withdrew into a shell where he felt safe, and couldn't take part in family activities or show affection. When visitors arrived he would stay for a while, then go to his bedroom where he would be angry or cry until they had left.

These reactions can be more difficult if your partner was previously outgoing, affectionate and demonstrative, made most of the decisions and took the lead in the family and in your social activities.

Clinging and dependent behaviour

Your partner might be clinging and dependent and make you feel as though you have another child in the family or a relative staying with you. This is particularly distressing if, before the incident, they were confident and caring and you shared everything together. You might become resentful because you now have to make most of the decisions in the home and family and you have to take on new and unfamiliar responsibilities.

Sexual activity

The reactions of you both mean that any closeness or sexual contact might be unlikely. You might find an intense need for comfort and sex, but the physical and emotional responses of you both keep you apart (see pages 49 and 84).

But what about you?

Does anyone know or understand how difficult and distressing this is for you? You too can experience reactions similar to those of your partner. You feel angry, disillusioned, picked on, helpless and irritable. You are physically and emotionally drained and feel that nobody cares about you. But there are ways in which you can cope (see Chapter 7).

Children

Children can be immediate victims or experience reactions because they live with someone who is traumatized, and reactions will generally depend on their age and level of development. If children do not have the vocabulary and ability to express emotions, they will find other ways of expressing them, especially through behaviour.

Play

Children usually find it easier to act out their emotions through what they do rather than by what they say. Some become surly or aggressive and unco-operative, especially in the way they play or take part in games. They might invent new games, especially those involving violence, and want to play 'soldiers' or war-games or act out situations where there is an accident or violence. They might even take on the role of someone in authority such as a police officer, doctor or soldier.

> One small boy of four had been involved in a traumatic event and was playing with Lego pieces. He had a Lego figure of a man and had put a number of white blocks on top of its head. He said it was a man who had been hurt and the white blocks were bandages.

Some retreat into their own world, become quiet and withdrawn, lose their appetite, play on their own and shun contact with other children, even their own siblings and close friends. They might destroy toys and playthings and become stubborn, bullying, aggressive, demanding and disruptive.

Paintings and drawings

Some children express how they feel through paintings and drawings.

> A girl of nine years whose father was away in the Gulf War had drawn a picture and said it was 'Daddy as a soldier'. She put the drawing on her bedside locker next to her father's photograph and told her mother she would only take her drawing away 'when Daddy comes home'.

Perhaps she was acting out her anxiety and symbolizing her fear that he might not come home? Some will draw or paint violent and disturbing situations.

Fear

Children can be afraid of any changes, both threatened or actual: moving home or changing schools; parental arguments or a breakdown in their relationship with separation and divorce; a death in the family, including that of a pet. Whether involved in actual incidents or just hearing about or seeing them, children can be frightened of doing anything they associate with the event, such as getting into a car or on to an aeroplane. One little boy was told that his grandad, who had died, had 'gone to sleep', and was afraid to go to bed in case he died!

Blame and guilt

Children can blame themselves for changes which take place, even when it's not their fault, especially for problems between parents and in the case of sexual and physical abuse. They might feel 'it must be my fault, because I'm bad', and, where a parent is withdrawn or unresponsive, 'Daddy ignores me or is angry, so I'm to blame'.

Anxiety

Children can be extra-sensitive to criticism, to being ignored or to a change in a relationship, and might become clinging, demanding affection and attention, or reject others, including parents. They might reject offers of physical comfort or love and become increasingly anxious.

> A mother had been involved in an armed robbery where she worked. Nobody had been physically hurt, but her children became very anxious and worried about her. They did not want her to go to work and were distressed whenever she left the house. When she did go to work, her children would ask if she would be coming home!

Illness

Like adults, children can also experience physical and emotional reactions to trauma and develop stomach aches, headaches, tummy upsets, rashes, listlessness and be generally unwell.

It is a common misconception that children are too young to understand and are not affected by difficult experiences. They will be affected and will try to understand, even if not in the same ways as adults. They certainly need reassurance, understanding and love, and they might need help.

Professionals

If you are a professional or a trained helper and rescuer, you will have developed strategies for coping. You will probably be very busy during an incident and you have a job to do, so you make a conscious effort to suppress and control your reactions and get on with the job. It's easier to think of the dead as 'dummies' or dolls, or say, 'This is only the shell. The real person has gone.' But this was a real, breathing, living person, with relatives, a family, husband, wife or children, and it could have been you or someone you love. Self-identification with victims is common.

A police officer had to shoot an armed robber. This was devastating enough, but when he saw the body he was shocked because the man looked like and was the same age as his own son.

A fire officer who had been in an incident where children were burnt to death would get up in the middle of the night to see if his own children were still breathing.

If you are a professional, you are expected to cope; breaking down and crying would be inappropriate, especially if you have lives to save. You don't want to be seen as weak or inadequate and you don't want to let anyone down, including yourself. The uniform, having a sense of purpose, the 'macho' image of some organizations and individuals and the feeling of comradeship and support, all help you to cope. One method often used by professionals, and sometimes misunderstood by others, is the use of 'sick humour'.

A group of fire officers who had attended the crash of a fighter aircraft, which had burst into flames, later greeted each other by half-crouching, screwing up their faces, curling their fingers like an animal ready to pounce and saying 'Grrrrr!' When asked why they did this they replied that this was how the body looked in the cockpit!

Like all sick humour, this can be a useful if grisly strategy. Why is it used? Hopefully, not because of callousness or lack of caring, but because it takes the sting or needle out of what you are doing and it helps you to cope. Keeping busy, suppressing your emotions and reactions, avoiding thinking about what you are doing and using humour, all are useful strategies for coping, but you can't always use these, especially if the incident overwhelms you. Also, your emotions and reactions don't disappear: you might be avoiding the need to express them and they might emerge later.

These strategies are mostly used during and shortly after incidents, but other methods can help. Some will talk to colleagues: others will never mention it. You might talk to your partner, or say, 'I never take my work home.' But if it has affected you, is it possible not to take it home in some way? You are carrying it around with you.

A social worker said that she didn't feel it right to talk to her colleagues about how she felt, because 'they already have enough problems of their own and I don't want to burden them further'. She kept quiet and suffered bouts of depression and irrational anger.

Another social worker said she coped by shouting and screaming in the car on her way home and by talking to her cat.

Cumulative stress

'Cumulative stress' is the stress which builds up over a period of time. It intensifies physical and emotional reactions and, like a slowly inflating balloon, will eventually burst. It can be found in professional rescuers and helpers, doctors, nurses, social workers, clergy, teachers, airline staff, overseas aid-workers and in anyone who experiences intermittent or sustained highly stressful situations. Reactions continue to be suppressed, and this becomes not only a way of coping but a way of life. Emotional withdrawal continues and you might become cold and unsympathetic. The following reactions will intensify: isolation; an unwillingness to take part in family or community activities; irritability; irrational, unreasonable and angry responses; cynicism, insensitivity and apathy; self-blame; tearfulness; sickness and illness; feelings of hopelessness and depression. There can be a build-up of adrenaline and energy which emerges in the 'kick the cat syndrome'. You come home from work feeling angry and bitter, open the door, the cat greets you and receives a blast of anger for its trouble, or you direct your feelings at your partner or children. This is the inappropriate and unhelpful transference of an emotion from one experience to another situation. It might be helpful for you, but not for the cat or anyone else in the line of fire. As the stress increases, you have difficulty in making decisions and are unsympathetic and insensitive to the needs of others, and if this continues, your health breaks down and you find difficulty in coping with work, with home life and with yourself.

Living with Post-Trauma Stress is difficult for all concerned, and sometimes it seems as though there is nothing you can do. You feel there is little point in trying and that nobody can help. The next chapters hope to convince you that you can do something to help yourself and that there are people who care.

6

Coping with Self

Previous chapters have looked at *how* you might have reacted and the possible effects on you and those around you. The aim of this chapter is to look at *why* you reacted, to offer models for understanding and to suggest strategies for coping.

Having read the previous chapters, if you have PTSD you probably now understand your reactions more clearly, but this might not make any difference to how you feel or reduce the level of your reactions (for help and advice see Chapter 8). If you do not have PTSD, your reactions can be anything from mild and short-lived to acute and longer-lasting, without developing into PTSD. Perhaps you have been off work for a time, have had some difficulty in coping with home life and your reactions have affected your relationships, but you have coped. Others cope with you, or put up with you, and the expectation is that these reactions and affects are only temporary. They won't go away completely, but you feel that as time passes they will reduce and become memories you can cope with. You accept that you might be reminded of the incident, especially if it happened somewhere you need to visit such as a work environment or the place where the incident occurred. If you were attacked or mugged on your way home, or were involved in a car accident in a particular spot, every time you pass that place or go near it you might become anxious or worried and try to avoid it. Even if you don't have any problems going there, it can still remind you of what you experienced.

Alternatively, your life might have been disrupted. You don't know what is happening to you or why, and you have found it difficult to cope both with yourself and with others. And those around you have been unable to cope with you.

What if I was injured?

Physical injuries are likely to intensify your reactions, especially of anger and helplessness. If you were stabbed or physically assaulted, you experienced the initial reaction of fear, might have thought you were going to be injured or killed, then felt the terror and physical pain which intensified the belief that you might die. Any injury, including loss of physical security, is a constant, and sometimes painful, reminder of what happened. Also, injuries are physically and emotionally draining, making it more difficult for you to control, accept or cope with your reactions. So, if you have been physically injured, reactions might be more intense and recovery usually takes longer.

Coping

What can help you to cope? Remember the themes of this book:

- The incident initiated your reactions.
- Most people react in ways which are perfectly normal.
- Reactions usually diminish with time, but some will still persist.
- There are ways in which you can help yourself and others to cope.
- Help is available if reactions persist or continue.

You can help yourself by increasing your understanding of:

- the incident;
- yourself and how you have reacted;
- why you have reacted and what you think and believe.

Understand the incident

It was the incident which triggered the reactions in you, and if you had not been there at the time you would not have been affected. In spite of how you feel, you must get this clearly fixed in your mind and repeat it to yourself over and over again:

'I have been in a traumatic incident and it was the incident which triggered my reactions. Even if I feel it, I am not weak, wet or pathetic.'

Write this down on a small card, and carry it with you.

Read it and say it to yourself regularly, silently or out loud, at various times throughout the day: when you get up in the morning, at coffee or lunch break and before you go to sleep. The problem is that feelings can be deceiving and convince you that 'you are what you feel'.

60

- I feel frightened – so I must be weak or pathetic.
- I feel guilty – so I must be to blame.
- I feel helpless and hopeless – so I must be useless.
- I feel angry – so I'm losing control or going mad.

You should now shout out: *'I am not just what I feel!'*

Do you feel pathetic, guilty, useless and mad? It's easy to say it but, no matter how distressing, these are 'only' feelings. Of course feelings are real, and they can be extremely disturbing and overpowering. But they might not be true. You can experience terrible feelings of guilt, even when it's not your fault! The guilt is real but, even though you feel you are to blame, it's not true. You are not guilty. It's normal to feel helpless in a threatening situation, but because you also feel stupid it doesn't mean that you are stupid. Some people are stupid and don't know it or feel it! Of course feelings are important, but they are only part of what makes you a person. In a frightening situation, the normal and natural reaction is to be afraid, even if you manage to control the fear. It would be unusual, if not abnormal, if you were not frightened. Your fear is natural, but can be so powerful that it makes it difficult for you to hear this or believe it.

> A woman telephoned an author who had written about loss and, because he was away, she left a message with his wife saying, 'Just say, thank you for page 95.' When his wife asked what this was about, the woman said that her son had died two years ago and she thought she was going mad. After reading page 95 of the book, she realized she wasn't.

It wasn't a 'cure', but it helped her to know that, in a sense, there was nothing wrong with her. She had lost her son and what she was experiencing were normal reactions to that terrible loss.

It's easy to say tht reactions are natural and normal and that these are 'only feelings', but some incidents and experiences are overwhelming and devastating. Experiences such as sexual abuse, physical and emotional abuse, rape, torture, seeing horrific sights, threats to your life, war and combat and disasters of all kinds will have more disturbing and longer-lasting effects. But, try to accept this statement.

> Because you feel there is something wrong with you, it doesn't mean that there is.

Put the blame for your reactions on the incident, not on yourself.

But you say, 'I'm a human being, not a robot, so my reactions must depend to some extent on me.' Correct! Let's look at this.

Understand yourself and how you have reacted

Sometimes you are physically and mentally more vulnerable because you are carrying beliefs, thoughts, ideas and problems from other experiences:

- relationships;
- work;
- health;
- other personal matters.

If you are already having problems in a relationship and are upset and angry or feeling hurt and raw, these feelings you are already holding can affect your reactions to a further trauma, and sometimes you will feel, 'I just can't take any more!' If you are dissatisfied at work, are having problems with colleagues, have been criticized, threatened with dismissal or redundancy or are about to retire, these can make you more sensitive to other events. When you are unwell, have had flu or feel tired or depressed, your ability to cope will also be reduced and the 'fight or flight' reaction, mentioned in Chapter 3, becomes difficult. It's not easy to fight or run away when you feel physically and mentally exhausted. Bereavement, moving house, marital breakdown and divorce, getting married, a new baby, taking out a huge loan and financial problems, being bullied or harassed, disputes with neighbours, acute disappointments, receiving bad news, all increase your stress level and reduce your ability to cope with other experiences (see pages 46–7).

Understand why you have reacted

There are various theories about why you have reacted and they suggest ways of helping and coping.

Life-beliefs Theory

An American psychologist (R. Janoff-Bulman) suggested that you have three basic life-beliefs which you absorb from birth, like a sponge taking in water. They will affect how you interpret and react to your experiences.

Invulnerability

This is the belief that bad things don't and won't happen to you, only to other people.

When asked if he was afraid of dying, Woody Allen, the writer and comedian, is supposed to have said, 'No. I'm just not going to be there when it happens!' He was invulnerable! You know you could have a heart attack or an accident, but you tell yourself, 'It can't happen to me.' Living in this false sense of security means that when disaster comes to your door your world is shattered and you ask, 'Why me?'

Why did you react? Because your false belief that you were living in a safe and secure world has been challenged. You have been forced to consider your own mortality.

Purpose and meaning

Think about these two questions. Write down your answers.

- What is your purpose in life?
- What or who gives you meaning?

Your purpose is probably to live as well and as long as you can and to live as useful and good a life as possible. Purpose and meaning come from beliefs, religious or otherwise, but also from significant things in your life: your home, family and friends, work and colleagues, your garden, the dog, holidays and the weather. These are not just people or objects, but parts of who and what you are. They give purpose to your existence and a reason for living. Therefore, when bad things happen to you, or to them, you ask, 'Why?' You are not looking for a rational answer, but for some ultimate purpose and meaning, even if you don't believe in God. 'Why me?' 'Why did it happen to her?' 'Why have I survived?' A practical answer, 'It happened because you were there', is not enough, and without a satisfactory answer you can feel picked on, disillusioned and that life is meaningless and without purpose. You could, of course, say, 'That's life!' and become cynical and pessimistic.

Why did you react? Because a traumatic experience has challenged you to ask questions about the meaning and purpose of your life.

Self-esteem

Are you a reasonably good person? Of course you are! Well, at least as good as anyone else! If you were in a situation of crisis, you would do your best to cope, wouldn't you? Your self-esteem, self-image and self-confidence are important. But difficult experiences force you to ask questions. 'Did I do my best?' 'Could I and should I have done more?' 'I saved one person, but should have saved them both.' 'I'm pathetic. I shouldn't have broken down and cried.' Your self-esteem and confidence can plummet, and, especially if you have made mistakes, you believe that you are weak, incompetent and inadequate. You feel guilty and a failure.

This theory challenges you to consider the following:

- How far were your reactions influenced by the belief that it couldn't happen to you?
  But you are vulnerable.
- Who or what gives you meaning and purpose in your life?
  But you are not guaranteed these forever.
- Are you a competent and confident person who always does what is right?
  But you can't always do what you want to do and you can make mistakes.

You say, 'Life shouldn't be like this,' but it is. You are not Superman or Superwoman, but a mortal and fragile human being living in an unpredictable world where difficult and distressing things can and do happen. This is a fact which challenges you to re-evaluate yourself, your beliefs and your life.

Bereavement Theory

On page 5, the SAD grief model of Shock, Anger and Depression was briefly outlined. The theory is that throughout your life you have to adjust to and cope with the many changes and resulting losses, both good and bad, which life brings, including bereavement. Sometimes adjustment is easy, but at other times extremely difficult. If someone you love dies, you don't say, 'Well, never mind. Next please!' Your reactions will be acute and long-lasting but, no matter how distressing, they are natural and necessary and not optional extras. You might try to 'get over' the loss and push it aside, but this doesn't work. You become stuck and can only move on to healing and renewal when you try to 'go through it'. You need to accept what has happened and allow reactions to emerge so that the experience is gradually absorbed and integrated into your life. It becomes part of you. You might feel, 'I want this experience to go away, as though it had never happened.' The fact is, it has happened and won't go away. You cannot 'cure' grief by forgetting about the person you love and you cannot get rid of the pain of trauma by putting the clock back or pretending that it didn't happen. Time is not like that. Neither are you and nor are your experiences. You have to live with them, no matter how painful. The challenge is this: will you try to push them away and forget them, or will you face up to them and work through them?

This theory suggests that in order to cope with trauma, you should try to accept that:

- the reactions you are experiencing are natural and mostly necessary;
- reactions are painful, because you have experienced a major change and loss in your life;
- reactions should not be ignored, but accepted and worked through;
- your life has changed and you need to adjust, and this will be difficult;
- you can begin to live with the experience, even if the pain and distress return;
- it will take time.

Crisis Theory

A 'crisis' is usually seen as something dramatic and bad, but the word comes from the Greek word *krisis*, where it means 'to separate', 'to decide' or 'judgement'. *Krisis* is a time of judgement and a challenge: to weigh things in the balance; to put things in order of priority; to decide what to believe and what to do. It is a turning point in your life, like a junction in the road. You can either stop where you are or make a choice about which way to go, and move on.

Crisis Theory suggests that when you face a difficult experience certain things happen:

- You try to suppress your painful feelings and emotions and keep them under control, but they won't go away.

- The natural balance between your mind and body is upset.
- There is a need to restore the balance and make the experience part of your life.

The theory is that there should be a natural balance in you between your body and mind. Your body represents your emotions and feelings: 'I had a gut feeling about that', 'I've got butterflies in my stomach', 'I can feel it in my bones.' Your mind represents your rational thinking: 'Use your head!', 'Think it through.' Although this division is a false one, it can be useful for thinking about why and how we react. Think of yourself as a pair of balancing scales. On one side is the 'feeling you' and on the other side the 'thinking you'. As you go through life, depending upon what is happening to you, each side swings up or down. When something traumatic happens, the balance is upset and usually comes down heavily on the side of feelings and emotions. You might be confused and attempt to think rationally and logically, but the tendency is for your emotions to take over. The event almost disappears and all that matters is how you feel, and you usually feel awful. You believe that you are what you feel (see pages 61–2). The need is to restore the balance so that the 'emotional you' and the 'thinking you' are as level as possible on the scales.

Exercises

The purpose of these exercises is to help you to try to restore the balance between your cognitive, thinking, rational self and your feeling self. They should not be too distressing.
   Don't try them if:

- You have severe reactions or PTSD.
- You think you might be more upset than you can cope with.

If in doubt, make sure someone you trust is near.
   Stop if it becomes too distressing.

Exercise 1
Have a pencil and paper for taking notes. Go through each of these stages and take it slowly.

What happened during the incident?

Try to stay in rational, thinking mode. Go through the facts, rather than allowing your feelings to dominate. Tell yourself what happened.

Calmly *think* and *talk* yourself through the incident from *before* it began *until it was o ʼer.* Making notes can help you to be more clear.

What feelings were generated by the incident?

Divide a sheet of paper into two from the top down the middle. On the top left half of the page, write *Feelings/reactions*, and on the right-hand side, *Reasons*. (See the example below.)

First, under *Feelings/reactions*, make a list of the feelings and physical reactions generated by what happened, e.g. shock, fear, helplessness, anger, shaking, fast heart-beat, etc. Allow a wide space under each one.

Then, under *Reasons*, write down what caused or triggered them. If in doubt, when looking for a reason, being your answer with, 'I reacted like this because . . .'

For example:

Feelings/reactions	*Reasons*
Fear	It was unexpected, the man had a gun and he threatened me.
Shaking	Because I was frightened – see above.
Thumping heart	Because I was frightened. Adrenaline rush. Need for oxygen, energy, etc. This made the fear worse.
Helplessness	The gun frightened me and I thought I could be killed, so I did nothing.
Anger	Because it was so unfair. He had no right to do that to me.

Look at your list and make sure you understand how and why you reacted. Note that there were reasons for your reactions. Therefore, because of what happened to you, your reactions were natural and normal. Be clear in your mind: you are not weak or pathetic for reacting as you did at the time or for being as you are now.

Support

Think about any support you have and who you have already talked to. Could you talk to them again if you needed to? Will you?

The here and now

Bring yourself right back into the present. Be aware of anything going on around you. If you need to, take a few deep breaths and then breathe normally and easily, get up, walk around, or make a cup of tea or coffee, and relax.

If you think it will help, talk to someone about the exercise.

Exercises 2 and 3

Read these through first. The same rules apply as for Exercise 1. *If you think they will be too painful or upsetting, don't do them.*

Exercise 2

Write down an account of your experience, from beginning to end, including the facts as well as your feelings. Read it to yourself regularly at the same time or times each day. If it would help, have someone with you when you do it and either read it yourself or ask them to read it to you. Note your reactions. With experience you should eventually be able to read it or hear it without becoming too disressed.

- What feelings do you remember? Make a list of them.
- Also, remember the facts because they triggered your reactions.

Exercise 3

Make an audio-tape recording of your experience, from beginning to end, including the facts as well as your feelings. Listen to the tape regularly. It might help to listen to it at the same time or times each day. If it would help, have someone with you when you do it. With experience you should eventually be able to hear it without becoming too distressed.

- What feelings do you remember? Make a list of them.
- Also, remember the facts because they triggered your reactions.

Exercise 4

Using your own reactions and feelings, try the 'Feelings/reactions – Reasons' exercise on pages 66–8.

Understand what you think and believe

The first-century philosopher Epictetus said that how you react to an experience will be determined not just by what happens, but by how you view and interpret it. You see a pint glass with half a pint of water in it. One person says it's half full and another that it's half empty. The quantity is the same, but being an optimist or a pessimist will influence your interpretation. If you believe the world is bad and that you are useless, when you have a traumatic experience you will probably fail, and this will confirm your beliefs that you are useless. What you think and believe determines what you see and say and affects how you behave. These thoughts and beliefs are usually about yourself, the world around you and the future. For example:

Belief/thought	Result
You:	
I am weak and pathetic.	You feel inadequate and you fail.
I am strong and confident.	You do your best.
I can't do it. I'm a failure.	You give in. You are a failure.
I can do it.	You succeed. More confidence.
I should have done more.	Guilt, anger, frustration, remorse.
I did all that I could.	Feeling you did your best, even if you couldn't do everything you wanted.
The world:	
The world is a bad place.	Fear, disillusionment, apathy, aggression, depression, withdrawal and isolation.
The world is basically good.	Relative happiness and security.
The future:	
Nothing matters any more.	Feelings of hopelessness – failure.
There is a reason to live.	Sense of purpose – achievement.

Using the above as a guide, write down your own list of beliefs and results.

The power of thoughts and beliefs to influence how you feel and behave is enormous.

Yourself

Think about these questions. Write down your answers.

- What did you believe about yourself and the world *before* the incident?
- What do you think about how you reacted at the time?
- What do you think and believe about your reactions now?
- Have any of your beliefs changed and, if so, in what ways?
- Would you call yourself a pessimist or an optimist? Why?

Even when you have done your best, you can still come out of a traumatic experience believing that you did not do enough: 'I should have been able to do more!' If you tell yourself that you have failed, you will probably conclude that you are useless.

Guilt and failure

You look back over your life and say, 'I could have done things differently, and if only I had, then life would have been better for me and for others.' This is known as 'the phonly syndrome', because 'phonly I had done this', and 'phonly I had done that' – 'If only!' Thoughts like these can lead to lack of self-esteem, guilt and depression. Ask yourself why you did what you did. There will be reasons. (See the exercise on page 67.) You might feel guilty or a failure because you didn't do something, but, under the circumstances, could you have done anything differently? Perhaps you could, but be aware of the difference between 'should' and 'could'. 'Should' implies you had a choice, 'could' suggests it was possible. You know this, but still say you 'should have' when you know that you 'couldn't have'. Well, you could have, but you might be dead!

Exercise

Reframing

Reframing is a technique where you try to look at your experience from a different angle. It attempts to change your interpretation of an experience, not the content.

Imagine the following scene, and that you are the person out for a walk.

Ask yourself the questions and make up possible answers:

> You are walking on the banks of a very wide, fast-flowing river. You see two young boys playing on the other side and one falls into the river shouting for help. *You cannot swim.* There is no bridge and no life-belt or rope. The boy is swept away and drowns. You are left with a deep sense of shame, guilt and remorse. 'If only I had been able to swim, I could have saved his life. It's my fault he died.'

Questions

- How did you feel during and after the incident?
- Why couldn't you swim?
- What did you do? What could you have done? What couldn't you do?
- Bearing in mind you couldn't swim, could you have done more?
- You say, 'I could have saved his life.' Do you mean 'I should have been able to'?
- What would have happened if you had dived in to try to rescue him?
- Even if you couldn't do what you wanted, did you do all that you could at the time?
- If you had drowned, what would the consequences be now for those you love?
- Who was responsible for what happened?

Your answers might not change everything, but they can adjust the way you interpret what happened and how you see your reactions.

Take your own experience and apply the same approach, asking similar questions.

- Why did it happen?
- What did you do and why?
- What did you not do and why?
- What would have happened if you had done something different at the time?
- What could, not should, you have done differently and what might have been the consequence?

- Who was responsible for what happened?

Coping with flash-backs
(See page 39.)

You might be having flash-backs: physical sensations, thoughts, images and feelings from the incident. They might be triggered, or some 'out of the blue' and be either mildly uncomfortable or terrifying. Where do they come from and why?

You have in your mind a vast store of images, thoughts and feelings from the past, and difficult memories, like good ones, can be recalled from the cupboards of your mind. If you look at a family photograph album, feelings begin to emerge and you feel happy or sad, laugh or cry, depending on the incident. The smell of daffodils or the sound of a voice might resurrect good memories and feelings. The sound of a police siren or the sight of a person might create panic and fear. But, remember, they are 'only' feelings! (See pages 60–2.) You can try to avoid them, and this might be a useful strategy, but this is not easy if your wife, home or place of work triggers the reactions. Experiences and reactions to them are there inside you, and deliberately trying to avoid them might not work, because they come whether you want them to or not. But, you can be stronger if you confront what you fear. With severe reactions this can seem almost impossible and you might need professional help to cope with them. What can you do if they do come and you can't stop them? If you can bear it, try this technique.

Exercise

When you feel the reactions coming on, relax as much as possible, breathe easily and steadily and at the same pace. Don't hyperventilate! If you can bear it, and you might not be able to stop them, allow the images and feelings to come. Control your breathing and say to yourself very firmly but calmly, repeating it if necessary,

> 'You cannot kill me. You are real, but, no matter how disturbing, you are only a feeling, a thought or a picture in my mind. I can survive.'

Keep breathing steadily and try to stay relaxed.

Alternatively you try to push them away by doing something, and this can help, but, no matter how disturbing, flash-backs cannot kill you, unless you panic and run under a no. 6 bus! Read the books by Claire Weekes recommended at the end of the chapter.

Conclusion

These theories all suggest similar ways of coping:

- Accept that the incident was responsible for triggering your reactions.
- Believe that your reactions are natural and normal.
- Burying feelings and emotions can have negative effects.
- Keep a balance between what happened, the facts, and how you reacted, your feelings.
- Emotions and feelings are important, but can be misleading.
- You might need to reassess what you think and believe.
- Working through your experience will probably be difficult.
- You can help yourself, but there are also other people who can understand and help.
- Try to see your experience as a challenge rather than a disaster.
- It will take time.

I know it is easy to say these. To believe them, when you feel terrible, is another matter. But life was never meant to be easy. It's a struggle. You know that better than most.

Believe in yourself.
Have faith in yourself.

You have been through and are going through a difficult time. Understand that those around you are also finding it difficult. Talk to them. Help them to understand you and give them support and love. Try to understand them and accept their love. If necessary, look for help and advice.

You will find other suggestions about coping in the next chapter.

References

Janoff-Bulman, R., 'The aftermath of victimization: rebuilding shattered assumptions', in Figley, C. R. (ed.), *Trauma and its Wake*, volume 1, Brunner Mazel, New York, 1985.

Weekes, Claire, *Peace from Nervous Suffering*, Angus and Robertson, London, 1972.

Weekes, Claire, *Self-Help for Your Nerves*, Angus and Robertson, London, 1988.

7

Coping with a Partner

How do you cope if you are living with someone who has experienced a traumatic incident? It can be anyone living with you in a close relationship, including a partner, husband or wife, parent, brother or sister, son or daughter or someone sharing a house or flat.

You might be coping well and feel that you don't need any help, and reading this book might have given you reassurance. You understand what has happened, you know how it has affected you and you have some idea why. But, even if you are coping, you realize that the experience can continue to affect your partner, with the possibility of flash-backs, dreams or nightmares and the triggering of reactions such as anger and irritability. You will probably continue to cope, but you might sometimes need support or advice. 'Be prepared!' is a good motto.

Are you finding it difficult to know what to do, what to say, or how to cope? Do you feel that nobody cares about you? The focus can be on your partner, particularly if the incident made the news headlines. This can also happen in a family, where all the attention is heaped upon the victim. The ripple effect of trauma can be forgotten: that it spreads out from the centre and, like flu, can be 'catching'. You might be ignored or just expected to get on with it. 'After all, look what it's done to poor old George!' You feel out on a limb and ask, 'Does anyone understand how difficult it is for me?' If you try to talk about or express your own needs, you might be accused of selfishness. 'How can she say such things when you see what has happened to George?' Does anyone understand what it's like to live with someone who can be angry and aggressive, irritable and demanding, cold and unloving, who talks incessantly about the incident or doesn't speak at all? Even if these are infrequent and mild, they can still be difficult to cope with. And what about your own reactions? Is anybody aware of these? You too can experience reactions similar to those of your partner: you feel angry and irritated, isolated and lonely, unloved and neglected. You might reach the stage where you are at the end of your tether! Remember, reactions for you, like those of your partner, can be anything from brief and upsetting to severe and distressing, but they usually reduce as time passes. Give yourself time! But there are things you can do to help. The following is general advice, but seek advice from a professional, especially your GP, if reactions and symptoms intensify or persist. Make sure you read the previous chapters, because they should increase your knowledge and understanding.

General advice

Some of these apply to you and your partner.

Understand what has happened

Make sure that you know what happened during the incident and when it was over. If your partner will not talk about it, find out from other sources, from friends, work, colleagues, the police and the media. You will find it easier to help and understand if you know what your partner has been through.

Understand what is happening to your partner

Ask yourself the following questions. Writing down your answers can help.

- How is your partner behaving?
- What feelings and emotions are being expressed?
- What are the physical reactions?
- Is it the expression of negative thoughts and beliefs? What are they?
- How long has it been going on?
- Is it resurrection of reactions some time after the incident?

Have you discussed these with your partner? If not, why not?

Understand what is happening to you and your family

Ask yourself the following questions. Writing down your answers can help.

- How have you reacted to your partner's behaviour?
- How has it affected you emotionally?
- How has it affected you physically?
- What things do you find difficult to cope with?

- What are your feelings?
- Does anyone understand how you feel and have you any support?
- How have the children or other family members been affected?

Have you discussed these with your partner? If not, why not?

Try to be as certain as possible about your answers. You might also try the 'Feelings/reactions – Reasons' exercise (see pages 66–8), using your own reactions and reasons.

Treat your partner normally

Unless there is physical injury, your partner is not ill so do not act like a nurse with a patient, even if that's how it feels. Be as natural as you can. Your attitude should be:

'You have been in a traumatic incident, but you are not ill. We all need time to recover. I can help, but you can also help yourself.'

Give reassurance of the normality of reactions, and also of your love and support. If appropriate, say that it will not be easy and that, with understanding, love and compassion, you will all cope. You and your partner must work together, and if you need help to do this, look for it.

Don't run away from your emotions

Tell yourself that your reactions are also normal. You say, 'I shouldn't be feeling like this.' But if you feel angry, then that's what you feel, so own the anger and accept it. It's real and it's yours! Don't run away from feelings and don't try to suppress them all the time. You might think, 'I have to be strong for all of us,' and sometimes you have to be calm and in control, but not all the time! One recurring theme in this book is that keeping your reactions, feelings and emotions locked away permanently is not usually helpful, because they can fester away inside until they explode. Find some way of expressing them and releasing the tension. You probably wouldn't want to start screaming or shouting in the local supermarket – but so what? If you did, it wouldn't be the end of the world! Sometimes you have to control your feelings, but don't be alarmed or ashamed if they do burst out now and again in unusual places. Unhelpful waiters and shop assistants are good targets! Find a safe place where you can express how you feel. Vent your anger in the privacy of your own home or expend the energy by doing something. If it helps, have a really good tantrum on your own: express how you feel verbally and physically by shouting and screaming, and if you are into swearing have a good swear. It can help to release tension and emotions and is better than nagging at your partner or children. You might not be comfortable with this advice, particularly about the swearing, so if it offends you, forget it. But it might help!

Listen to your partner

Listen to what your partner is saying. If there are particular themes, what are they and what ideas or beliefs lie behind them in your partner's mind? Can you do or say anything to help? Be careful not to collude by allowing the constant talking to become an obsession, where your partner repeats the same things each time but never seems to get anywhere. Realize that you can only take so much and sometimes you have to say to yourself, 'I've had enough for now. I know it's important for you to talk, but I need a break.'

How to respond when listening

Don't just say, 'Um! Yes! Uh! Uh!' all of the time, but respond actively. But:

> Try not to get into an argument.
> Do not be aggressive or dismissive.
> When necessary, be quite challenging.

If something is said which is clearly not true or is highly questionable, say so very clearly and firmly and be intensely practical and honest (see pages 70–2, 'Reframing'). Your partner makes a statement:

Statement: 'I must be weak and pathetic for not helping. I should have done something.'

Response: 'Look, you couldn't do anything because if you had you might have been killed. You would also have put other people's lives at risk.'

78

Make sure this is heard and if necessary repeat it in a different way, perhaps by making a statement and asking a question.

Response: 'You said you should have done something. The man was threatening you with a gun and could have killed you. Tell me exactly what you could have done, and what the consequences might have been if you had.'

Don't allow this statement and question to be ignored, but repeat it again if necessary. Concentrate on the facts of what happened – what could and couldn't be done and what was done – and challenge 'should have done' statements.

You can make an even clearer statement or question.

Response: 'Look, I'm trying to understand. You say, "should have done something". If you had, you could be dead, I could be grieving, your children could be without a father and your funeral would be this week or over by now. Is that what might have happened? Perhaps you didn't do anything because you were afraid and knew this?'

Challenge statements which are debatable or not true. You are trying to put another angle on how your partner interprets what happened. Where they are mentioned, acknowledge feelings sensitively, but don't allow them to overshadow your response. The feelings could be of guilt, helplessness or survivor-guilt, and that needs to be understood, but these feelings come from what happened in the incident, so acknowledge the feelings.

Response: 'You are feeling awful and guilty about what happened. You felt so helpless at the time and you still do.'

But don't forget the facts:

Response: 'You were helpless at the time and feel guilty about what happened. But you did have a gun pointed at you. How did that make you feel and what could have happened if you had done something?'

You won't get it right all of the time, especially when you are trying to cope with your own feelings as well as with those of your partner. Be prepared for an angry cry that you don't understand. It needs some courage and thought to do it, but *try it*. What you say and how you respond can help. You are attempting to restore the balance between feelings and the facts of the situation as they were and are now.

Talk normally

Talk normally and naturally and don't be too protective. The world is still going on and the ordinary things of everyday life should not be avoided or ignored. When it feels appropriate, let your partner know what's happening to you. Say how it affects you and your family, how you feel and what you think, not aggressively or blaming but clearly and firmly. You might be reluctant to say how you feel in case your partner becomes more distressed and feels even more guilty or angry. You might feel guilty for saying it, but you need to be honest, both with yourself and with your partner. If you don't say it, it's still there inside you.

Don't say things that are unhelpful

The following might be true, but are not usually helpful:

- *'I know how you feel.'*
  The only person whose feelings you feel is you. You might know what they feel but not how they feel. (See pages 81–2, 'Offer sympathy and empathy'.)
- *'I coped. So should you.'*
  People cope in different ways, and some less successfully than others. Because you coped, it doesn't mean that others should be the same.
- *'Other people are all right, so what's wrong with you?'*
  Traumatic incidents affect different people in different ways at different times and no two people's reactions will be the same.
- *'But it wasn't very serious.'*
  If it was serious for your partner, then it is serious, no matter what you think.
- *'Pull yourself together. Get a grip on yourself.'*
  This is just what your partner cannot do. It implies that your

partner is weak, pathetic or wet, and even, for some reason or other, enjoying the misery!

- *'Don't you do that. I'll do it for you.'*
  This can take away self-confidence and give the impression that your partner is an invalid. Doing something takes effort and your partner might feel more involved, more in control and less dependent.
- *'Time is a great healer.'*
  This is usually true, but it can be unhelpful and inappropriate and give the impression that you don't really care or understand.
- *'There are others far worse than you.'*
  This is like telling someone who has lost a leg that there are people who have lost two. True, but not very helpful.

Avoid accusations

Do not say anything which might give the impression that you blame your partner, either for what happened or for the reactions.

- You are pathetic/weak/hopeless/wet/stupid/an idiot.
- There must be something seriously wrong with you.
- You are going mad.
- You are useless – as a partner/father/lover, etc.
- You should be over it by now.
- You can't do anything right.

Understandably, you might say these when you are upset, frustrated or angry, but they don't help.

Offer sympathy and empathy

Sympathy is not 'I know how you feel.' Not only is this not true, it is insulting and patronizing and shows that you really don't know. Sympathy can be saying, 'You must feel terrible,' or 'You seem to be very angry and that must be awful for you.' It means standing alongside someone to support them and saying, 'I don't understand, but I'm here.' Empathy is much deeper and is trying to feel, from your own experiences, something someone else feels. Your partner is frightened, so you recall a time when you were afraid and try to get in touch with it, but you realize that this is your own fear and not theirs. Try to understand how your partner feels. This doesn't mean putting up with everything your partner says or does. 'I realize you are very upset, but it doesn't help when you shout at me.' Your partner also needs to understand and respect your feelings.

Be available – but not too available

Be around to help, but do not 'hover'. You have your own life to live. Trauma victims can be very demanding and clinging; if you are too available you can take responsibility away from your partner and confirm the feelings of helplessness and inadequacy. Don't take over and do everything. You can only do so much before you become exhausted. Look after your partner, but also look after yourself!

Cope with feelings and forgive yourself

Don't allow your own feelings or those of your partner to dominate your life. Anger, guilt and resentment can churn away inside and influence everything you think and do. Remember that you are also affected by what has happened and your partner is not the only one trying to cope. Things will be said and done which you both regret, but that's life! You are not perfect, but trying to do your best to cope in a difficult situation.

Coping with anger and violence
(See also pages 38 and 51.)

Upsets and arguments can be acceptable because they are normal and natural. Bouts of anger and frustration will usually be directed against objects such as crockery, ornaments and furniture rather than at you.

When you react to anger:

- Respond at a level slightly below that of your partner.
- Try to stay calm. Be firm. Be assertive. Stand up for yourself.
- Do not allow the anger to crush you.
- If necessary – walk away.

Verbal anger might be tolerable, but physical violence is not. With physical anger:

- Stay calm. Say clearly that this behaviour is unacceptable.
- Say what the consequences will be if it continues.
- If it becomes dangerous and risky, leave and *seek help*.

You, and any children, should not accept living in a violent environment.

Ask your partner to do things

Ask your partner to go shopping or to do things around the home. You should not be doing everything, but sharing in running the home and looking after the children. This establishes that everyone has a role to play and a responsibility in the relationship. It can also help to restore lost confidence and to regain feelings of independence, involvement and control. (See page 81, 'Don't you do that. I'll do it for you'.)

Take care of the children
(See also pages 53–5.)

The children will react to your partner's reactions and to yours, and to the atmosphere created. They might behave strangely and out of character and become very difficult to cope with. They will need reassurance, extra love and understanding; if they are old enough, tell them what has happened and explain that it will be difficult to them and for you all for a while, but that things will get better.

Cope with withdrawal

A traumatic expereience can cause you and your partner to draw away from each other physically and emotionally so that you both feel isolated and alone (see pages 52–3). Carry on the basics of caring and use some of the strategies suggested in this chapter. Give reassurance of your love, but also give yourself space and time.

Have time for yourself

Do not become housebound or victim-bound. Keep up your own hobbies and interests, especially those different from your partner. Keep in touch with your friends and talk to them, but don't become a bore, always talking about your partner and your problems. Take plenty of exercise and mentally and physically look after yourself. Give yourself a treat now and again. A large bar of chocolate might be a good idea!

Find someone you can trust and talk to them

You must look after yourself. If you don't need to or want to go to a professional, talk to someone you can trust who will try to understand you and not criticize you. Share your concerns and feelings with them. Ask yourself:

- Who have I talked to since the incident and can I continue to talk to them?
- If not, is there anyone else?

Sex isn't everything!

Well, it isn't, is it? It is important, but you can't always have what you want! Don't be surprised or disappointed if you find that sex goes out of the window for a while. You might even be relieved not to have the extra pressure, especially when you and your partner are mentally and physically exhausted from trying to cope with a host of difficult feelings and reactions. You are trying to cope with yourself, your partner, work, the children and running a home, and there might be no warmth or closeness. Is it any wonder there is little or no sex? You need to give yourself and your partner time to adjust. If your partner is clinging and needy, this can either turn you on, turn you off or leave you cold. On the other hand, you might have an increased sex life and feel a deep need for physical closeness, comfort and relief.

Use a 'mantra'

This book has suggested that your partner should use a 'mantra' every day. You also can have one. Make up your own, write it down on a card and say it when you get up in the morning and regularly throughout the day. Choose something like:

'I am trying my best. It is not easy for my partner, and it is not easy for me. But I can cope and I will survive.'

Other strategies for coping

Use any of the strategies and exercises suggested in Chapter 6 and Chapter 8. Do not look for miracles, but expect that things will gradually improve. If they don't, look for help.

8

Looking for Help

Help comes through understanding what has happened to you, knowing how you have reacted and why, and believing that you can help yourself. There are self-help strategies you can use outlined in Chapter 7 and here, and also many organizations and individuals who will offer advice and support. If one doesn't work or help, try another.

Helping yourself

Join a support group

A support group should consist of those who have had similar, but not necessarily the same, traumatic experiences. If group sessions don't work for you, look elsewhere.

Self-help exercises

If you haven't done them, try the exercises on pages 66–9 and the 'Reframing' exercise on pages 70–2.

Exercise and diet

Exercise and diet can increase your general health, physical fitness and self-confidence. You local surgery will let you have a diet sheet.

Prayer and beliefs

You don't have to be religious to pray. The French philosopher Voltaire, in the eighteenth century, had strong views against organized religion but was seen raising his hat as he passed a church. A friend said, 'I thought you didn't believe in God!' Voltaire replied, 'We are not on speaking terms, but we do acknowledge one another.' Prayer is not simply about asking for things, but more about acknowledging that there is, or might be, some greater power and opening yourself up to that possibility. Make time to re-think what you believe about yourself, other people, the purpose of life, the world around you and your future. Try talking to a clergyman, or read a book on religion and beliefs.

Visit the scene of the incident

If you can, go to the place where the incident occurred. If necessary, take someone with you for support. This can help you to face up to your fears and the memories and give you a sense of achievement and self-confidence.

Yoga and meditation

Look for a local class or group or find a suitable book. For information contact:

Yoga for Health Foundation	Tel: 01767–627271
British Wheel of Yoga	Tel: 01529–303233

Relaxation classes and techniques

For information about relaxation classes and techniques, contact:

The Stress Management Training Institute   Tel: 01983–868166

Audio-tapes are available in some shops and are best used with personal stereos. Most are based on learning to gradually relax your body while listening to a voice telling you what to do, usually with music in the background.

Your local surgery or library might lend relaxation tapes and CDs. They can be purchased from some local shops or from:

New World Music Ltd   Tel: 01986–781682
The Barn
Becks Green
St Andrews
Beccles
Suffolk
NR34 8NB

Listen to music

Listen to your favourite pieces of music using a personal stereo or personal CD player.

Acupuncture, reflexology and aromatherapy

Alternative therapies of many kinds are worth trying, but might be expensive. Remember, if you believe in it enough, it just might work!

Stress management courses

If you can find them or afford them, attend a stress or anger management course. If the problem is through work, your employer might pay.

Laughter

Laughter is a good medicine. It might be difficult to do, but try it. Watch your favourite comedy programmes or comedians on TV or on tape. Recall times when you were happy and enjoyed life. Find something about yourself to laugh at!

Help others

Helping others can help you, and many charities look for volunteers or part-time helpers. Your local Citizens' Advice Bureau will give you names and addresses to contact.

Help at work

Some people at work might not know about or acknowledge the effects of stress and trauma and some might be quite sceptical or critical, but there will be people, departments and agencies offering help and advice. If they can't help, they should point you in the right direction. Obviously, you will only contact these if you feel you can trust them. Some organizations offer help automatically when there has been a traumatic incident through Defusing, Debriefing, counselling and referral to various agencies. Those who should offer assistance are:

- human resources and personnel departments;
- your line-manager or supervisor;
- occupational health staff;
- welfare officers – usually also trained counsellors;
- staff support help-lines – usually a confidential telephone line;
- Employee Assistance Programmes (EAPs) – an outside agency offering confidential help and counselling, sometimes paid for by your organization;
- professional consultants: psychiatrists and psychologists;
- counsellors, sometimes full-time employees or from external agencies;
- chaplains and clergy of many denominations and religions.

Defusing or Critical Incident Debriefing might be offered following incidents at work, or you might seek Debriefing privately. This is a procedure aimed at helping you to look at what you have experienced and the reactions generated, and to give you information about resources for helping. It can last from three to four hours and is not counselling.

Your GP, hospitals and clinics

Your first point of contact should be your doctor. The surgery should have a counsellor available and, at your GP's suggestion, a CPN (Community Psychiatric Nurse) might become involved. You can ask to be referred to a local clinic where you would see a psychologist or psychotherapist. Cognitive-behavioural therapy, which looks at patterns of thinking and learned behaviour, seems to work best for most people. It might help just to talk to an impartial helper or counsellor.

Not every GP understands Post-Trauma Stress or PTSD, and you might be offered medication for anxiety, depression, insomnia or some other condition. These can help, but you might need to treat the cause rather than just the symptoms. If you are not satisfied, look elsewhere for advice.

Children with problems

Your GP can refer you to a specialist. Also, through the school, ask for advice from an educational psychologist.

Hospitals and clinics

Contact your surgery or telephone your local hospital and ask if they have a department of psychiatry or psychology and what they can offer. Some have a local support group. The following are only a few of the hospitals and clinics available and most have to be accessed via your GP. There should be others in your area.

The Traumatic Stress Clinic

Will take UK-wide referrals from your GP.

73 Charlotte Street, London, W1P 1LB
Tel: 020–7530 3666

The Traumatic Stress Clinic

Institute of Psychiatry   Tel: 020–7919 3458
The Maudsley Hospital
de Crespigny Park
Denmark Hill
London
SE5 8AZ

Departments of Clinical Psychology

Ask your local surgery or hospital about any clinics available in your area.

- Withington Hospital, Manchester M20 8RL Tel: 0161–2914058
- The Warneford Hospital, Oxford OX3 7JX Tel: 01865–741717

Ty Gwyn

21 Bryn y Bia Road   24 hour help-line: Tel: 01492–544081
Craigside
Llandudno
Gwynedd
North Wales
LL30 3AS

The Rivers' Centre

29 Morningside Park   Tel: 0131–537 6797
Edinburgh
EH10 5HF

Private hospitals

If you have medical insurance or can pay, you can be referred to a private hospital. They can be expensive.

Ticehurst House Hospital

Ticehurst   Tel: 01580–200391
Wadhurst
East Sussex
TN5 7HU

Ticehurst Clinic

Hove   Tel: 01273–747464
East Sussex
BN4 4FH

Duke's Priory Hospital

Stumps Lane   Tel: 01245–345345
Springfield
Chelmsford
Essex
CM1 5SJ

The Ridgeway Hospital

Wroughton   Tel: 01793–814848
Swindon
SN4 9DD

Organizations offering advice and help

Any of the following will offer you advice and help and, in some cases, counselling. If they can't help directly, they will point you to someone who can.

For ex-service personnel

The Ex-Services' Mental Welfare Society (Combat Stress)

They have welfare officers in regions throughout the country and also offer advice, respite and treatment. Obtain your local contact from:

The Ex-Services Mental Welfare Society   Tel: 01372–841600
Tyrwhitt House
Oaklawn Road
Leatherhead
Surrey
KT22 0BX

War Pensioners' Welfare Agency

Help-line: Tel: 01253–858858

The Defence Services' Psychiatric Centre

Duchess of Kent's Hospital   Tel: 01748–832521
Catterick
North Yorkshire
DL9 4DF

The Royal Naval Hospital
(Probably closing in 2002)

Department of Psychiatry   Tel: 023–9258 4255
Haslar
Gosport
Hants
PO12 2AA

Soldiers', Sailors' and Airmen's Families' Association and Forces' Help

19 Queen Elizabeth Street   Tel: 020–7403 8783
London
SE1 2LP

Veterans' Advice Unit

Tel: 08456–020302

Other Organizations

Some of the following are nationwide organizations with branches in every town or city. Your directory will give you the local telephone number, or contact the number given.

Citizens' Advice Bureaux

An invaluable local resource offering help and advice and local and national contact numbers. Look in your local directory for the telephone number.

Victim Support

They will visit at your request and have a system for supporting people who have to go to court as witnesses. Contact telephone number in a local directory or through:

Central Office   Tel: 020–7735 9166
Cramer House
39 Brixton Road
London
SW9 6DZ

The Salvation Army

The Salvation Army Counselling Service   Tel: 020–8771 9244
18 Thane Street
Kings Cross
London
WC1H 9QL

Assist

General advice and counselling help.

The Penthouse   Office: Tel: 01788–551919
11 Bank Street   Help-line: Tel: 01788–560800
Rugby
Warwickshire
CV21 2QE

The British Association for Counselling

Offering experienced trauma counsellors in every area of the country. Explain it is for Post-Trauma Stress and they will give you names and telephone numbers to contact.

1 Regent Place	Office: Tel: 01788–560899
Rugby	Information: Tel: 01788–578328
Warwickshire	
CV21 2PJ	

Mind (National Association for Mental Health)

Granta House	Office: Tel: 020–8519 2122
15–19 Broadway	Information: Tel: 020–8522 1728
Stratford	
London	
E15 4BQ	

Relate

Not specializing in Post-Trauma Stress but offering general counselling. Local group in telephone directory or contact:

National Headquarters	Tel: 01788–573241
Herbert Grey College	
Little Church Street	
Rugby	
Warwickshire	
CV21 3AP	

Cruse

For bereavement.

126 Sheen Road	Tel: 020–8940 4818
Richmond	
Surrey	
TW9 1UR	

Rape crisis centres

Local groups available or contact through London headquarters:

PO Box 69   Tel: 020–7837 1600
London
WC1X 9NJ

Male rape

There will be contact numbers in your local area, or ask Citizens'
Advice Bureaux.

Trauma Aftercare Trust (TACT)

Buttfields   Help-line: Tel: 01242–890306
The Farthings
Withington
Glos
GL54 4DF

Post-Trauma Stress, Critical Incident Debriefing and counselling

For help, advice, conselling, Critical Incident Debriefing and
training, and can offer referral to people in different parts of the
country.

British Association for Counselling See page 93.

Frank Parkinson

Priory Associates   Tel: 01793–784406
9 Priory Mead
Longcot
Faringdon
Oxon
SN7 7TJ

Carole Spiers Associates

Gordon House   Tel: 020–8954 1593
83–85 Gordon Avenue
Stanmore
Middlesex
HA7 3QR

Centre for Crisis Psychology

Four Arches   Tel: 01756–796383
Broughton Hall
Skipton
North Yorkshire
BD23 3AD

Counselling or therapy

Do not be put off by the words 'counselling', 'therapy', 'psychologist', 'psychotherapist' or 'psychiatrist'. A professional counsellor or therapist is not a 'do-gooder' poking into your private life and will not tell you what to do, but will help you to look at and make your own choices and decisions. Cognitive-behavioural therapy with a counsellor, psychotherapist or psychologist can help with trauma, and other methods of counselling are used for personal matters. If you have more than one name to contact, check them all, but be sure to ask the following questions:

- What training, qualifications and experience do you have for helping me with my particular problems?
- What techniques or methods do you use?
- If private, how much do you charge?
- Will I be committed to a certain number of sessions?
- Can I have one session to see how we get on?

As a general rule:

- Get your impressions from the person's voice and manner.
- Do not commit yourself to a set number of sessions.
- Try one session first, because you might not get on with the person or like the approach used.

- Do not look for miracles or magic wands.
- Accept that it will probably be difficult and might be painful.

With any of the suggestions in this book, use the following rules:

- If it doesn't work, try something else.
- Don't give in. Keep trying.
- There is help and there are ways through what you are experiencing.
- Remember that you didn't ask to be traumatized.

You might discover strengths and resources inside you which you never knew existed.

Further Reading

Stress and Post-Trauma Stress

Bennet, Glin, *Beyond Endurance – Survival at the Extremes*, Secker and Warburg, London, 1983.

Bettelheim, Bruno, *The Informed Heart*, Penguin Books (Peregrine), London, 1986.

Cooper, C.L., Cooper, R.D. and Eaker, L.H., *Living with Stress*, Penguin Books, London, 1988.

Everstine, D.S. and Everstine, L., *The Trauma Response – Treatment for Emotional Injury*, John Wiley, Chichester, 1993.

Greener, Mark, *The Which Guide to Managing Stress*, Which Books, London, 1996.

Herbert, C. and Wetmore, A., *Overcoming Post-Trauma Stress*, Robinson, London, 2000.

Kinchen, David, *Post-Traumatic Stress Disorder*, HarperCollins/ Thorsons, London, 1994.

Marks, I.M., *Living with Fear*, McGraw-Hill, London and New York, 1980.

Parkinson, Frank, *Post-Trauma Stress*, Sheldon Press, London, 1993.

Parkinson, Frank, *Listening and Helping in the Workplace*, Souvenir Press, London, 1995.

Parkinson, Frank, *Critical Incident Debriefing*, Souvenir Press, London, 1997.

Rowe, Dorothy, *Beyond Fear*, Fontana/HarperCollins, London, 1987.

Scott, M.J. and Stradling, S.G., *Counselling for PTSD*, Sage, London, 1992.

Tedeschi, R.G. and Calhoun, L.G., *Trauma and Transformation*, Sage, London, 1995.

van der Kolk, B.A., McFarlane, A. C. and Weisaeth, L. (eds), *Traumatic Stress*, Guildford Press, New York, 1996. (Expensive and academic, but useful.)

Weekes, Claire, *Peace from Nervous Suffering*, Angus and Robertson, London, 1972.

Weekes, Claire, *Self-Help for Your Nerves*, Angus and Robertson, London, 1988.

War and combat stress

Holden, Wendy, *Shell Shock*, Channel 4 Books/Macmillan, London, 1998.
Keegan, John, *The Face of Battle*, Pimlico, London, 1991.
McManners, Hugh, *The Scars of War*, HarperCollins, London, 1993.

Bereavement and loss

Lake, Tony, *Living with Loss*, Sheldon Press, London, 1984.
Lewis, C.S., *A Grief Observed*, Faber & Faber, London, 1961.
Pincus, Lily, *Death and the Family*, Faber & Faber, London, reprinted 1997.
Raphael, B., *The Anatomy of Bereavement*, Routledge, London, 1984.

General reading

Adams, A., *Bullying at Work*, Virago Press, London, 1992.
Curtis, L., *Sexual Harassment at Work – How to Cope*, BBC Publication, London, 1993.
Goleman, Daniel, *Emotional Intelligence*, Bloomsbury, London, 1996.
Keenan, Brian, *An Evil Cradling*, Vintage Books, London, 1992.
Skynner, Robin, and Cleese, John, *Families and How to Survive Them*, Methuen, London, 1987.
Skynner, Robin, and Cleese, John, *Life and How to Survive It*, Methuen, London, 1993.

Novels

Barker, Pat, *The Regeneration Trilogy: Regeneration*, *The Eye in the Door* and *The Ghost Road*, Viking, London, 1996.
Faulks, Sebastian, *Birdsong*, Hutchinson, London, 1993; Vintage, London, 1994.

Index